Judy Jackson

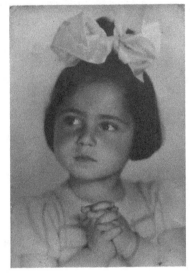

Monika Sears

First published in 2019 by Marsons

Printed in Great Britain

Text and cover design by Rachel Jackson | binahdesign.com

Authors: Judy Jackson and Monika Sears

A CIP catalogue record for this book is availabe from
The British Library.

ISBN 978-0-9517220-7-7
www.marsonsbooks.com

*For our seven sons
and their sons and daughters*

episodes

two girls, two lives—one time

BY JUDY JACKSON & MONIKA SEARS

introduction

The stories of the two young girls in this book were written long after the events. Without consulting each other, they simply wrote what they remembered about the period from 1939 when they were born, to 1950 when they first met. It began when Europe was in the turmoil of war: one girl was swept into the terror of Nazi occupied Poland, while the other grew up in the relative calm of living in London during the Blitz.

Monika was born in Lódz, Poland in February 1939. Judith was born in London, England in June 1939. How did they end up meeting at the gate to St Paul's school? Their childhoods could not have been more different.

One might think that the two girls had almost no common ground in their early years. For many months Monika (then called Marysia, or Mary) was left alone in a room all day, hidden under a table, while her mother went to work to earn money to bring back small amounts of food. At no time was Judith hungry, nor did she ever face the panic of being confronted by armed men in uniform.

Yet their early memories show surprising similarities and a young girl's humiliation or embarrassment is something never forgotten.

Life for Mary, sent to a school where she couldn't speak or understand the language, held many terrors. These were compounded by continued fears of being hungry or chased, with a constant need to find a hiding place. The English child merely had to contend with travelling across London to a school in a new environment, sharing a classroom with pupils who seemed to come from a different world. Both girls were far from happy.

This is the story of the eleven years before they met at the gates of St. Paul's Girls' School. They became friends from the first day. They each changed their name: Mary reverted to the name she was given at birth, Monika. Judith preferred to be known as Judy.

In all their conversations in the cricket nets and on the tennis courts, they never talked about the Holocaust in Poland or the Blitz in London. Looking back on it, as she saw her own children grow, Monika realized that she had not had a childhood. Whilst other girls worried about lost gym bags and obeyed the school rules and regulations, she had found it difficult to take notice of instructions given by someone who was not wielding a machine gun.

Part 1 is their wartime experiences. Part 2 follows their lives at separate junior schools, until they met for the first time, beginning a friendship that was to last a lifetime.

Judith's story, containing those memories she can unravel of her early years, was all written in 2018. It is told first from a child's viewpoint, then from that of a girl growing up. Monika's Part 1 is written more in the language of an adult, but without any history of the period or analysis of the horrors being perpetrated. Originally it took the form of a letter to her first grandson, written shortly after his birth in 1981. It was then translated into Italian and finally published as *From My War to Your Peace* in 2016.

Both accounts reflect what was known and felt at the time. At the bottom of some chapters is a clarification of what was actually happening, called *What I Now Know*.

Inevitably the pain and problems of that period still remain vivid. Recent conversations have helped to soften the memories and illuminate the emotions they evoked, lending them a kinder perspective.

part 1

1

London 1941—Judith

I was about two and a half, getting ready to go to a birthday party. The clothes were laid out on the bed: a smocked dress with short puffed sleeves, white socks and buttoned-down patent leather shoes. I wriggled as my mother fixed a ribbon in my hair. My father had been putting a picture on the wall, knocking a nail in with a hammer. He left the hammer on the table.

My brother David came into the room and started pulling at the ribbon. He was nearly two years older than me. Older brothers have annoying habits. He couldn't get a grip on my hair which was short and curly, so yanking at the ribbon had the desired effect of making me squeal.

Maybe other children would have given him a pinch. I saw the hammer and without thinking, picked it up and brought it down on David's head. A line of blood trickled from his forehead. He took a long breath and then started to cry. His screams reached the neighbours' garden. They probably stopped watering their potato plants.

The ribbon was on the floor; it was entwined with a few strands of my hair. David kept sobbing as he fingered his bruise. I was crying too. We didn't go to the party. My mother went to find Witch Hazel and plasters.

My father put me in the push chair and wheeled me out of the house, along Walm Lane and up the hill. When we got to Lydford Road he put the brake on so we could stay on the bridge and look down at the railway line. My father said very little. We watched as several trains passed and stopped at the station. When I got tired of this I said I was ready to go back. David wasn't around. My mother was ironing a pile of linen. I rushed into her arms and it was then that I began to understand what I had done.

I heard her explaining that a head wasn't like a ball, but more like a fragile bubble, and then we noticed a smell of burning. The iron had singed a dark yellow mark on the pillow case. My father took my hand and we went to read a story.

Warsaw 1941—Marysia

I was about two and a half. We were in the ghetto, a place where Jews lived. There were shows for little children and I saw my cousin on a stage with a group of other children, reciting a poem about a huge radish or parsnip that wouldn't come out of the ground. They all pretended to pull and I was almost frantic with jealousy. I must have made a fuss, because they passed me over the heads of the audience and I recited a poem, all by myself— and to my enormous satisfaction—about a locomotive that went choof-puff.The applause was nothing more than I deserved and I felt I had scored off my cousin, who had to share her applause.

We lived in a flat and from the balcony I watched my mother hurry away. I slept with my two cousins in one bed, and the sheets and the blankets and the walls all had the greeny-yellow tinge of the one weak light bulb in the room. I knew not to cry or complain: I was never told about that. We stayed in bed to keep warm and we didn't cry or whine. There are shadowy faces of adults, always huddled, whispering, afraid, feeding us but never talking to us because that wasn't important. If there was a knock at the door there was a scuffling of secret things being quickly hidden, sometimes under the floorboards, sometimes under the blankets where we three children sat.

I went somewhere else with my mother. She came to fetch me and carried me away. There were always the dreaded uniforms, and they were always everywhere.

What I Now Know

My mother married my father when she was twenty four. Pavel was considered quite a catch, being the son of Moses Rozenfeld & Co. hosiery manufacturers of Lódz. When the German army invaded Poland, they had a system of taking away the richest and the best-known members of the Jewish community—and making them disappear without trace. My father was one of them. Morale collapsed. Rumours flew. On the strength of one of these rumours, my mother went from Lódz to Warsaw, taking food, money and her baby. She never saw her husband again. He was then thirty three years old.

2

London 1942—Judith

Does childhood memory go back to the age of two or three? What I recall now are flashes of my life as a young child. We lived in Cricklewood in a road called Walm Lane, with a church at one end and the shops at the other end. Every day a milk cart came round and I think there was a bread van, but I preferred it when we went to the shop to buy those loaves which were crusty outside and soft in the middle. I loved the smell and the warm feeling when I got to hold the paper bag. There were other carts trundling along: one piled with sacks of coal. The men had thick oily hoods and carried the sacks on their shoulders and tipped the coal into the bunker in the back garden.

In the evenings we had to be careful to draw the blackout curtains. Wardens walked round to see if you had pulled them right across the windows; otherwise they would shout 'put that light out.' There were no lights in the streets either.

My grandfather and aunt lived not far away in Mapesbury Road. Walking into their house was like stepping into a different kind of darkness. The rooms were all brown, with dark tables and a piano covered with a big knitted shawl. We never had a meal there. There were photograph frames with pictures of my grandmother, stretched out on a chair which my father called a 'chaise-longue'. This must have been when she was resting because she had had a stroke. I didn't know what that was and wondered if it had anything to do with stroking kittens. I can't remember ever seeing her. Perhaps she had died before I was born.

We often took a trolleybus to go to see my other grandmother who lived far away in Finchley. Sometimes there would be thick fog and we couldn't see to cross the road when we arrived at the right bus stop. She opened the door wearing a long black dress with a lacy white collar. Her white hair was piled on top of her head. She had a soft face and her skin smelt sweet as she bent down to kiss me. She would untie my woollen pixie hat that fastened under my chin to keep out the cold winter winds.

My father also had white hair—but it was wispy and his head was shiny at the top. I don't know what fathers were supposed to look like, but I have an idea that he must have been different from the others. When we went to the bank he would sit me on the counter and give me slips of paper to play with. The man behind the desk would sometimes hand me the new cheque book and say 'Give it to your Grandpa.'

Around my birthday there was a lot of talk about the new clothing ration. You couldn't just go out to a shop and buy a dress or a coat. You needed to have a book with coupons. I heard a story that a family went on a train to Scotland with their two children. They put the luggage in the guard's van and when they got to Edinburgh the suitcases were no longer there. Someone had stolen them. Inside were all the clothes the family owned. Their

Scottish cousins all helped by collecting coupons and sharing them so they could buy new dresses, coats and trousers.

My father didn't care about new clothes. He liked to wear crumpled trousers and a battered old hat. He wore a tweed jacket, a tie and a freshly ironed shirt. Every Sunday he sat on a stool in the scullery and covered the floor with newspapers. Then he started to clean his shoes. He used an old cloth to put on a black paste and then a brush to make the shoes shiny. Finally he took a clean, yellowy cloth which was soft and rubbed it back and forth over the front of the shoes to make them shine. I think he had three pairs of shoes and he did them all, each week.

What I Now Know

The Clothes Ration: Around a quarter of the British population was entitled to wear some kind of uniform as part of the armed forces. The demand for these uniforms put enormous pressure on Britain's textile and clothing industries. Clothes rationing was introduced to improve the availability of items in the shops and to make sure they were distributed fairly. Payment was made with points and money.

The Blackout: Britain was plunged into darkness at sunset on 1 September 1939, two days before war was declared. (The Air Ministry had predicted that in the event of war, night bombing attacks would cause large numbers of civilian casualties. So as early as July 1939, public information leaflets were already being circulated.) Street lights were switched off at the mains, vehicle headlights were masked to show only a crack of light and stations were lit by candles. All windows had to be covered at night with heavy curtains, cardboard or paint, to prevent the slightest glimmer of light that might help the enemy aircraft to identify a town.

Warsaw 1942—Marysia

My mother had bleached her hair an improbable corn gold. I heard her say it looked passably Aryan. I didn't understand that or talk of 'a lot of money' 'leaving the ghetto' and 'buying forged identity papers good enough for us to survive on the other side'.

She sewed at a machine in an enormous room with a lot of other women, and I sat under her machine, keeping out of the way of the pedal and keeping silent. It was important to have work, because the Germans took people away if they were young and weren't working. She once told me what they were all making, but I can't remember. I remember looking at the legs all working their pedals, and then sitting on a stone staircase drinking something hot and delicious and being grabbed and pulled out of the way of a number of booted legs coming up the stairs. I lost my drink and cried, and a hand was put over my face. Where we lived I can't recall at all.

At about this time I must have been made to understand that my mother wasn't my mother at all but a very nice lady who looked after me, and I was to call her Ciocia Krysia—Auntie Krysia.

Auntie Pola was to look after me too. Pola was a young, bright peasant girl who worked for the family as a nursery maid before the war. She stuck with my Mother through most of the war and, when things became intolerable, took me off to the country, passed me off as her bastard, and got herself labouring work. When things became too difficult for her, she took me back to my Mother, and so the ping-pong went on. The reason why things got difficult for each of them in turn was always because I looked 'wrong'. To look 'right' at that time you had to be able to pass as an Aryan and not have people look questioningly at you.

We were in a large palace occupied by Germans, but here they were mostly relaxed and laughing, and they sometimes pinched my cheeks. I had a thick black and red check coat made out of a blanket, a white woollen pixie hood and warm boots, and I was sent out to play in the snow, out of the way of the kitchens. In a compound was an injured baby deer that some of the German soldiers were nursing, and I was allowed to feed it and pet it. There was one soldier who was a special friend of Pola's, and he made me a toboggan and pulled me up the hill. He took me to the compound and held the little deer so that I could stroke it and feed it from the bottle, which it tugged at vigorously. He carried me on his shoulder.

The kitchen where Pola worked was vast, with a huge, old-fashioned kitchen range where I sat quietly, out of the way, when I could no longer be kept outside. Winters in Poland are very cold. I was given bowls of peas to shell and potatoes, already peeled, that had to have the odd eye or scar taken out. Sometimes the cook would put two or three dry beans on the hot range for me and I would watch them jump up and down and dance. Then one day, the kitchen door opened and a tall officer in immaculate grey uniform and shiny boots stood flushed and laughing in the door frame, holding an enormous silver salver in his hand. The people working in the kitchen fell silent.

"I'm told there is a child here." he said. That could only be an accusation. I made myself very small and tried to shelter behind the woman working at the stove. She stepped sharply to one side. Perhaps he spoke Polish, though this is unlikely. Perhaps everybody understood the word oKindo. I know that I understood he was looking for me. He came over to me, very handsome and jolly, and lowered the salver. On it was one large slice of cake with piped cream. "Eat" he said. I looked up at him, disobeying every instruction I had ever been given. He pointed to the cake. "Eat! Eat!"

Pola, some way behind him, was smiling. I took the cake and ate. Someone clapped, and then everybody clapped. The officer gave a curt bow and left. I don't remember the taste of the cake, but I remember that the piece was so large I had to hold it in both hands and the cream stuck to my nose and mouth.

What I Now Know

The dangers of being Jewish or harbouring a Jew: For a Pole, harbouring a Jew meant death with no extenuating circumstances. A little Jew like me was therefore a time-bomb both for Auntie Krysia and for Pola, for I couldn't have looked more 'wrong'. The Poles are almost uniformly Slavic in appearance. The armies that have invaded and devastated their country over the centuries have left very little legacy of dark brown hair and huge, sad, brown eyes. In a field of fair hair, blue eyes and high cheekbones, these were the marks of a Jew. My hair was streaked with gold lights and I was taught always to look modestly down, especially when talking to people. What was taken for charming, childish shyness, was merely a survival tactic.

Until well after the end of the war I was sometimes with Auntie Krysia, sometimes with Pola. I learned afterwards that Pola had hoped to marry her German soldier and that, in order not to be compromised by a bastard child, she had told him the truth about me. The result could have been disastrous, but in the event all I can remember is laughter and kindness from him.

Years later I discovered how much Pola had been paid to keep me alive and how the rates kept going up.

3

The house where I lived was cold but bright. It had two big rooms downstairs at the front that were 'for best': the dining room with walls made of dark brown wood and the living room with velvety green chairs. They were only used once a week and my father had to turn on electric fires from early in the morning to make them warm. At the back of the house was the kitchen. It had a boiler, a pulley to hang clothes, and a big wooden table in the middle with upright chairs that scraped on the tiled floor. Down a few steps was the scullery where there were sinks and a cooker. If it wasn't supper time it always seemed to be even colder down there. My favourite room was the little sitting room, with a few comfy chairs and a coal fire. As a special treat we sometimes had Friday evening dinner in there. I loved to watch the flames shooting up in the fireplace.

A few streets away from the house was my first school: St. Helen's. I don't have any memory of my first day there or how I passed the time in the first year. I expect we played but quite soon we were made to sit at desks and listen to the teachers.

One day when my mother fetched me at half past three, she told me a story as we walked home. She had been cleaning the steps in the front of the house, using a special paste to brighten the stone. A man walked past and asked her how much she was being paid. He offered to pay her more if she would come and work for him.

I don't know exactly how my mother spent her time. While I was doing sums and practising my handwriting in a lined book, I believe she was getting food for us. She went to queue at the local shops, handing in our ration coupons and looking to see if there had been any new deliveries. She hadn't seen any onions for weeks. I didn't care about the onions; sweets were more important. Looking for these was something we did together, after school, but the extra shopping trip was also just in case there was anything else to be found.

As we got near the corner bakery there was a smell wafting out. That was the fresh bread. I hoped we'd join the queue at the sweet shop. My mother usually bought some Passing Cloud cigarettes for my father and tried to find a threepenny bag of toffees and tiger nuts for me and David. My ration book was green (for a child) and I didn't understand then what 'the two-ounce allowance for the week' meant, but I did realize that the bag was not very full.

When I got home my father was feeding the chickens. That made a revolting smell. He had a blade fixed to a long pole and was chumping a mixture of left-over porridge and potato peelings. (I expect he wasn't the one who stood over the pan as they were cooking in the scullery). As he mashed up the hot grey mess, I was pulling at his trousers, asking if I could look for the eggs. He let me put my hand under a pile of straw and pull out one brown egg.

What I Now Know

Keeping chickens: During the war eggs were rationed. To add to the very few fresh eggs that were available, you could buy pickled eggs, stored upside down in a pail filled with sodium silicate. There was also a dried egg powder which came from the USA in 1942. It had a long shelf life but an unappealing taste and texture. People started keeping chickens in their back yards, but, there was a catch: you had to give up your egg ration in return for a grain ration to feed them.

The countryside near Warsaw 1943/44—Marysia

The servants didn't sleep in the palace, and other than the kitchen I don't think I ever saw any other room there. The outside was white and sprawling, and to me, at least, was obviously an enchanted castle with a sleeping princess or two up in the attic rooms with the small windows in the roof. There was a dairy and just next to it a number of cottages—or maybe just huts—where we slept. I slept with Pola on a straw-filled mattress, and every now and then we would empty it and put in fresh straw. This was a painful process, but I was proud of the scratches I had, which made me the equal of Pola, and very brave. (One night the women gathered pine-needles and put them in the men's mattresses. I remember the hushed excitement, but not the consequences.) I don't remember Pola's smile or her praise, but I do remember her anger and that I loved her. Sometimes I would wake up in the night and she was not there, and I know I was frightened of the shadows and the straw poking out of the mattress, which could be mischievous and alive in the dark. But I lay still and didn't try to look for her or cry, because her anger would have been more awful than any phantoms that the mere night could conjure up.

I didn't know what the clear liquid was called, but there were bottles of it on the table with the evening potatoes. Pola would push me down as soon as I had eaten and hold me in an iron grip between her legs under the bench. Even so, I wasn't always forgotten and when the call came to produce 'the bastard' I was hauled up. That was a different kind of fear. They put me on the table and made me dance. They taught me songs I didn't understand, with alternating lines in Polish and in German. They clapped wildly as I pranced among the plates and the bottles, holding my skirt prettily at the side and warbling the ditties I had so quickly learned by heart. I was rewarded with sips from a bottle. I enjoyed making them all laugh and clap, without understanding why. I was also very afraid to stop, and Pola wouldn't let me come down.

The palace complex was also a small working farm, run for the benefit of the illustrious occupants. We ate potatoes and sour milk. There were chickens, and when their heads had been chopped off they were let loose to run round the farmyard until they dropped. Sometimes they ran into the shallow, fast-flowing stream that bounded one side of the yard. They then had to be pulled out again, amid much shouting and laughter. Goose, duck and chicken feathers were collected and sorted to make pillows and quilts for the officers. My fingers were small and nimble, and I picked the down. There were feathers flying round the room and sometimes it was difficult to breathe. Sometimes I was given a little scrap of chicken to eat. We didn't sleep on feather beds.

I was ill. I had mumps and then chicken-pox. I was taken into another cottage and put in a bright room with a feather bed. Pola had to go to work, so she left water and milk for me by my bed. When the chicken-pox arrived, I had evidently not had time to recover from the mumps, for I can still recall what an effort it was not to cry or make a noise. My hands were tied to the bed so that I would not scratch my face and leave scars. Often the sun shone directly onto the bed. Then I was better and the weather was warm. I had clogs, like everyone else, and I ran about the farm and in the woods near the palace. Everywhere was very green. There was no-one to play with and nobody had time to talk to me, but nobody paid any attention to me either, so I did what I pleased.

Of course I had been told many times that I must not go anywhere near the dogs chained to the kennels. There were a lot of them in the grounds, and they belonged to the Germans. Sometimes I watched the soldiers feed them, keeping my distance from both soldiers and dogs.

Perhaps I misjudged the length of a chain or perhaps I was being naughty: whichever it was a Dobermann which a moment earlier had been snoozing in the sun, suddenly came flying through the air towards me.

I remember being back in the feather bed with a priest looking down at me and Pola—a grown-up—crying. Then, to my eternal shame, I was lying on the warm grass, wrapped in newspapers. Apparently I had blood poisoning and had nearly died. Pola had burnt all my clothes to fool the spirits, so they would think I didn't exist and would go away. It obviously worked, for I recovered. They took me, all wrapped in newspapers, to the dairy and shot milk straight from the udder into my mouth. I recovered from that too. Motley clothes appeared and I was able to play in the fields and clap when the headless chickens ran round the yard. Once the delirium was over they took me out into the sunshine. Pola was with me a lot, and when she was not there a surly shepherd-boy kept an eye on me. He didn't like my chatter. He found it humiliating to be looking after a child, because the others laughed at him.

The harvest saw everybody in the fields. There were other children around then and we were all set to picking up what was left after the women had gathered the corn, so that not one ear should be left behind and wasted.The stubble was sharp and made deep gashes in our legs. We looked for the 'pepper pots' left by the poppies and were encouraged to eat the seeds. All the other children knew each other and were not impressed either by the handsome gashes I had on my legs—at least equal to theirs—or by the songs I could sing. Most of the time I worked behind Pola and accepted that these wonderful creatures would want nothing to do with me. After the harvest was in, I didn't see them any more.

What I Now Know

The dancing child: I can still sing the odd line of the songs and now know how obscene they were, especially in the mouth of a child. The bottle contained vodka and I was no doubt frequently drunk while I was dancing on the table.

I suppose Pola realized that the Polish servants of German masters had their own anger and frustrations and that it would have been dangerous to spoil their fun, once they had decided that the fun for the night was to be a drunken little girl. Perhaps she enjoyed the fun herself. I'll never know. She was young, and the burden of having a 'bastard' foisted on her must have been very heavy at times.

Pola's fears: Not only was it awkward to have an illegitimate child, but the sneers about the race of the father—only too obvious from my appearance—were becoming dangerous. I think she hoped to marry her little German soldier. Pola could not keep me any longer. So I was taken back to Warsaw, to Auntie Krysia.

4

My mother had a help I called Beatis. Her real name was Beatrice. I loved to sit in the kitchen and talk to her while she was doing the ironing. There were piles of sheets and bolster cases and tablecloths with my parents' initials embroidered in the corner. Beatis told me about her husband Jack who worked for the Post Office and her son Bernard who wanted to join the RAF. These airmen were very important people. They flew the planes that were defending us from the Germans.

We were used to the noise of the planes and the air-raid warning. The sound got louder and louder—an insistent booming that made everyone scurry around. We had to rush into the air-raid shelter outside the back door of the kitchen. I heard people talking about Anderson shelters, which were outside, and Morrison shelters, which were really like big tables, inside. My grandfather, who lived in a house a few streets away with my aunt and their maid called Maria, had one of those. Three people had to squeeze in underneath the gigantic iron table until the threat of the bombs had passed.

We grabbed blankets and food and rushed inside the dank, dark space. David and I clambered into our bunks giggling. We thought it was fun. When the All Clear sounded, we went back indoors and my father would leave immediately. He was on Fire Watch and had to walk round the local streets checking to see if any of the houses had caught fire. Then he had to go to the local Fire Warden and report what he had seen. He was often quiet when he came back. He whispered to my mother that he'd seen whole houses disappear. I couldn't understand that. Disappearing was magic. I think he was talking about something called 'rubble'.

My mother was good at sewing, as well as cooking. I don't know how she learned to do smocking, but she made me pretty dresses with matching knickers.

Before the war she had been a teacher—maths I think—but she told me later she didn't like the atmosphere in the staff room and decided to start a business making chocolates. She taught herself how to do something called 'tempering'—nothing to do with a bad temper, like David sometimes got into, but mashing the chocolate till it was smooth. Then she had tools for dipping and marking and fillings called fondant. When the war started you couldn't get chocolate any more. Sugar and everything else was on ration. There were no more proper home-made cakes as the butter ration was so tiny.

What I Now Know

Food rationing: At the start of World War II, Britain imported a high percentage of its food. Cheese, fats, meat, sugar and fruit nearly all came from abroad. The Germans had a strategy to attack shipping bound for the British Isles, aiming to restrict our industry and potentially starve the nation into submission.

The Ministry of Food instituted a system of rationing to deal with extreme shortages. The population of the country was about fifty million. Each person was sent a ration book containing coupons and had to register at chosen shops. The shopkeeper was provided with enough food for their specified customers. Purchasers had to take ration books with them when shopping, so the coupons could be torn out and handed over.

Air raid shelters: An Anderson shelter was by far the most common 'private' shelter. It was designed to be put up at the bottom of a suburban garden, and could hold up to six people.To be fully effective, the concrete shelter had to be dug into a 4ft deep pit in the ground, where it was covered with earth as protection against nearby bomb blasts. There were about three million of them. I think ours was put up by a rogue builder, because it wasn't dug into the ground, but simply placed on top. It was freezing cold and (for the adults) a deeply unpleasant place to be.

That's why the government developed a shelter that could be used inside the home. The Morrison shelter was effectively a metal cage, which doubled as a kitchen table. The shelters came in assembly kits with 359 parts and three tools. At least half a million of them were installed in private homes, giving protection till the air-raid subsided.

Auntie Krysia had found a room with a Countess, her daughter, and a grandson called Maciej. The Countess hated Jews and didn't like children, so Pola's decision to bring me back caused problems. Auntie Krysia could not confide in the daughter, Mrs. Rybicka, and was afraid of the grandson, who was about my age. He whined constantly and had a room full of toys and a balcony that overlooked the large communal gardens below.

Our small room was just to the right of the front door and faced the street. It had a bow window, so that it was possible to see into the equivalent room in the next-door flat, which had a similar window (it would almost be easier to draw a plan!). Next to our room was Mrs. Rybicka's bedroom. The Countess occupied what had once been the drawing-room, the dining-room and the kitchen, where she could oversee the stocks of food and dispense rations. Next to the kitchen, with his door exactly opposite our room, slept Maciej.

I was smuggled into Auntie Krysia's room. Pola and Auntie Krysia explained that there was a monster in the flat who was really a German and ate little girls. I must never be seen or heard. Above all, I must never, ever go to the window.

Against the wall there was a table and two chairs. Over the table Auntie Krysia draped a brown cloth or blanket, and here I stayed, in complete silence, while she went to work. I had a potty which Auntie Krysia emptied at night, and it was at night that she brought me hot food and a small bowl of water in which we would carefully wash each other. Once she left in the morning, I crawled under the table and didn't move until she came back. I had one or two picture-books, two toy armchairs and a little wooden table painted orange, and a rag doll. In the evening Auntie Krysia would give me two sweets, delicious soft toffees that melted in the mouth, wrapped in yellow and white paper with a picture of a little brown cow in the middle.

Auntie Krysia ate with the family—mashed potatoes and sour milk every night. Then it was her duty to read to the Countess for at least an hour. Then, and only then, was she free to spend a little time with me. Thus we lived for some months. It was cosy under the table and I was not afraid. Silence quickly became normal. I could not hear the outside world and nobody could see or hear me.

When Mrs. Rybicka knocked at the door and asked to come in, I knew I must not breathe. This happened quite often: I suppose she lacked company. Sometimes she brought Auntie Krysia a hot drink and one for herself and with this as an excuse she settled down at the table for a chat. I kept out of the way of her legs. Auntie Krysia slipped her hand under the table every now and then and stroked my head. Other than our landlady's lonely visits, nobody else came into the room.

It is hard to imagine it now, being hidden under a table for days, weeks, months at a time, with a few toys and picture books. Perhaps I slept a lot. I was very aggressive in defending my little kingdom. The sounds of Maciej running freely round the flat, of Mrs. Rybicka talking with her mother, and of shooting in the street were audible to me but made no impression. It was as if nothing could reach me when I was under the table, or as if I had ceased to exist. I was not impatient for Auntie Krysia to come home and, even when she did, I did not always rush out to the comparative freedom of our room.

On one or two occasions Pola came to visit Auntie Krysia and I sat in her lap, cuddled close. They talked as if I were not there and I felt important to be allowed to listen to such conferences. I begged to be taken back by Pola. She had nowhere safe for me. I could no longer be taken out into the street. She cried, so I cried. She coaxed me back under the table and went away.

Then there was shouting in the streets outside the window, and at night the sky was bright with chandeliers suspended by magic threads. It was very beautiful. When the bombing started, we all ran for the cellars and so my presence was discovered. The cellars were crowded and people fought for space. The Countess sat on a deckchair, but Auntie Krysia and I only had the floor and later a box. We could hear fires burning, and sometimes a door was opened at the top of a steep staircase and we could see flames across the street. As their own houses were burnt down, so the rats came to join us in our cellar, as yet untouched by the bombing. People hit them, but there wasn't much room and they seemed to settle in the places we humans could not use, on top of pipes and between storage boxes.

In the cellar I was presented to the Countess and bobbed a little curtsy, as I had been taught, with my eyes carefully lowered. She could not believe that we had been living all those months in the same flat without her having heard me. I was her dear child and a paragon of virtue—a silent child was the best sort of child, after all. Auntie Krysia told her I was an orphan and the child of her best friend. She said that she could not abandon me. The Countess approved of such loyalty displayed in the harsh conditions which they were all undergoing. She graciously offered to help my aunt. No back rent was to be charged for the months I had been in her flat as a stowaway; but, now that I could stay officially, join them for meals and become a little companion for Maciej, a proper consideration would be expected. I looked from one to the other and felt moved by my own plight. I had not known that I was an orphan. That, together with the approval of this haughty lady, made me feel very saintly. Orphans were usually the heroes of fairy stories and I wondered if it was Krysia or Pola who was to be my fairy godmother. There was no doubt that the Countess had the potential to be a witch. I had had plenty of time, under my table with my picture-books, to build a world of spells and magic, far away from the war. Sometimes I saw somebody who fitted into this world. Sometimes this led to confusion and I smiled when I should have backed away, or cried when a smile would have been helpful. The Countess should have been sweetened with a smile.

The bombing stopped and we went back upstairs. I was taken to Maciej's room and he was told to let me play with a toy. He couldn't think of one that he could spare even for five minutes. His grandmother chose a toy herself and handed it to me. Maciej wept inconsolably. I hoped he wasn't a prince in disguise and I didn't want him to find out that I was an orphan, just in case that magic knowledge turned him into my particular prince. I asked to go back to our room. I never spoke above a whisper, which the Countess considered a wonderful quality in a child. She scolded Maciej. He hated me at once and forever. He never failed to pinch, scratch or snatch when he thought he could get away with it, which was most of the time. He was the first child I had ever tried to talk to, other than the older children during harvest-time at the palace. I could not understand why he cried, when I knew that it was forbidden. Maciej's room was a magic cave full of toys and I would have been quite happy to sit and look, but the Countess insisted that we play and Auntie Krysia trembled lest some aspect of my behaviour should be found wanting.

These visits to Maciej's room were quite formal. Mrs. Rybicka or the Countess knocked on the door of our room and issued an invitation. I went across the hall, with a ribbon in my hair, accompanied by Auntie Krysia. The three women sat in upright chairs and watched us play. The Countess called me dziewczynka—the little girl. Perhaps she could not remember my name. Her instructions to Maciej came in a voice that brooked no argument: 'Give dziewczynka the train' or 'give dziewczynka the teddy bear.'

I would take the toy and sit with it in my lap, knowing that I must not move it or damage it and that it was too precious for me, since it would be snatched back by the owner as soon as the Countess began to talk to Auntie Krysia or to her daughter.

I was never invited if Auntie Krysia was out at work, and I continued to sit contentedly under my table, even though the need for secrecy had been removed.

It must have been at this time that the flat had another secret tenant, Mr. Rybicki had come back. When the banging on the door came in the middle of the night, Auntie Krysia was convinced it was for her and tried to hide me under the mattress. The soldier who pulled back the mattress hardly gave me a second glance as he threw me into the hall to wait with the others. I stood next to Auntie Krysia as the door of the dining-room opened and two soldiers triumphantly pulled out a bald, bedraggled man. They let him kiss Maciej before pushing him out of the front door. We stood in the hall in silence waiting for our turn. Mrs. Rybicka did not cry, and even Maciej was silent. That was the only time I saw Mr. Rybicki. They took him away and didn't come back for us, though we waited, listening for the familiar scrape of arrogant boots on the stone stairs. Both the Countess and her daughter treated us with a slight air of apology, but no-one came back for us, and the Countess very quickly settled back into her aura of faint disdain.

In the evenings I was now invited to join the family for dinner. This was always thin soup, potatoes and sour milk. The Countess put a very small knob of butter on Maciej's potatoes. Auntie Krysia and I watched with large, greedy eyes as it melted deliciously. Auntie Krysia had a jar of goose fat secreted in our room, and sometimes she spread some very thinly on a piece of bread for me. That was a deep secret, though: we were supposed to be a 'family' and share provisions. Some members of the family were obviously more privileged than others, and I was never honoured with a little knob of butter. Maciej never tasted the goose fat.

The trips to the cellar became more frequent and lasted longer. People fought. They accused each other of stealing. I never looked up at their faces, though now that I was under the protection of the Countess my breeding could not have come into question. The rats, quite as hungry as we were, grew bolder.

What I Now Know

The dangers of collusion: Mr. Rybicki was a high-ranking officer in the Polish underground. He was a prize eagerly sought by the Germans. The punishment for harbouring a partisan was death. We had thus been exposed to the fate the regulations prescribed for those colluding with partisans.

The sweets my mother gave me: The toffees I ate under the table are still being made and in London I sometimes go to a Polish shop and buy a whole bagful. I only ever eat two at a time.

5

Wartime—Judith

I often heard my parents whispering about the war, what was allowed and what wasn't allowed. They talked about where we could buy a herring, or any fruit other than an apple or a pear. I'd never tasted a banana, and oranges only appeared if a sailor was home on leave and brought a couple with him. We had no sailors in our family.

I'd never been to a theatre, but my father used to tell me about shows he loved, like Gilbert and Sullivan. Apparently just after the war started all the theatres were closed, but quite soon it was decided to re-open them because it would make the people happy.

There seemed to be no danger in going to learn dancing so my mother enrolled me in a class that was a few stops away from Kilburn tube station. I don't think it was ballet because I have no memory of little pink shoes with ribbons, but there might have been tap dancing because that was something you could do with your ordinary shoes. Mine were black shiny leather with a button—you needed a button hook to fasten them and take them off.

One day after the class we walked to the station and climbed the stairs to the right platform to go home. There was a strong wind blowing and I tightened my scarf and pulled on the mittens my mother had knitted. Standing on the platform I started to practise the steps I'd learnt that day: step side, step forward, turn, step back, kick... ...   As I stretched out out my right leg my shoe suddenly slipped off and I watched it rise in the air and then continue travelling till it came to a stop beyond the edge of the platform, down on the rails. I gave a shriek and clapped my hand over my mouth. My mother stood there, horrified. She called the station master and they stood there talking for a few minutes. I was mortified. How could I go home with only one shoe? And where would we get another one if we had used all our coupons?

I don't know how the lost shoe was retrieved, but some time later a crowd had formed and someone was coming over to us to give us something. I think I pretended it had nothing to do with me.

What I Now Know

Oranges were still in short supply even after the war. To make one last longer, my mother cut a square hole in the top and pushed in a sugar cube. Then we squeezed the orange, sucking out the juice and the sugar.

Wartime—Marysia

On the roof of the block of flats on the other side of the garden, a white flag appeared from time to time, and when that happened it was safe to go out. I was taken with Maciej to play in the desolate garden, sometimes by his mother, sometimes by Auntie Krysia. Other children were let out into the sun and I met another little boy whose name I can't quite remember any more; it may have been Bolek. Soon he came to the flat to play in Maciej's wonderful room and he knew all sorts of games. He was very bright and I think I must have been in love with him, because I insisted on walking hand in hand with him everywhere.

Warsaw was burning and the Germans wanted us out of our flat, as they were clearing the district. They banged on the door and told us we had to get out—immediately. We all went into the garden and waited to be told what to do. There were soldiers with guns stationed on the roofs, all the way round us.We were prodded into a semblance of a column and were herded through the archway out into the street. I walked hand in hand with Bolek. Auntie Krysia was behind us. The column moved very fast, and soldiers in boots and helmets were stationed on both sides of the road. There was a burning tram in the middle of the road and buildings burning everywhere. Soot clung to our eyelashes. I clung to Bolek.

Smouldering debris lay across our path, but nobody veered from the column.

Bayonets were used freely on stragglers and those who did not want to step over bits of burning rubble or dead bodies. There was a pall of smoke over the city and the stench of burning buildings and rotting flesh.

We were pushed into a vast hall under the arches of a road bridge.

A row of officers blocked off the other end. One of the officers stood on a platform and boomed in German through a large double megaphone. We were being given news and instructions. Warsaw was to be burnt to the ground and its citizens sent away. They were not ready for our buildings yet. We were to go back to our flats and await further instructions. The doors of the hall opened again and we were led out. I didn't understand any of this at the time: I just heard the voice.

We walked back towards our buildings. The column was very quiet. Every now and again a shot rang out and there was a scream. There were soldiers leaning against huge motorbikes and laughing. Bolek tripped and I pulled at his arm, but he didn't get up. Some of his clothes were torn and the insides of his tummy were hanging out. There was a hole where his coat used to button up, and blood. I knelt down next to him and with my hands I took all the insides and tried to push them back into the hole as fast as I could. Auntie Krysia pulled me away and I tried to explain to her that Bolek had fallen apart. She lifted me up and carried me, and I was angry that she had not let me stay to put Bolek back together again.

What I Now Know

The whole incident sounds horrendous, yet as a child I know I felt no revulsion. I knew about death and assumed that, if I could get all Bolek's intestines back into the hole, I could get him to stand up again and walk on. My anger was reserved for Auntie Krysia who prevented me from doing this. In retrospect, every moment of his death is clear, and also the bewilderment that somebody I knew and loved had ceased to exist. Until then perhaps, I had never realized that the corpses in the streets had once been people.

6

Wartime—Judith

The black nights continued. It made people sad. There were no twinkly lights and I think we were all a bit afraid of the ARP wardens. They seemed to have eyes everywhere as they went about their business, checking every window in every house. We all knew it was important to obey the rules.

Children didn't go out after dark but it seemed as if the grown-ups were having an adventure if they made a journey across the city in the evening. You couldn't see more than three feet in front of you, even with a good torch. I heard my parents talking about the rules and the dangers. The colour chosen to solve the problem was white. White paint was painted on kerbs and round the doors of tube trains. Farmers even painted white stripes on the cows so they could find them in the dark. Policemen dipped their capes and tunics in special paint so they could be seen. My parents said they looked like ghosts. I didn't know what these were.

What I Now Know

The Blackout: ARP meant Air Raid Precautions. The blackout curtains could not be washed, as water might have damaged their light-proofing. The government issued a leaflet telling people to "hoover, shake or brush them, and then iron".

There was a serious increase in deaths on the road and coroners urged pedestrians to carry a newspaper or white handkerchief to make them more visible. Many were killed stepping from the pub into a darkened street.

Even with a 20mph speed limit, car crashes were frequent. Traffic lights were reduced to tiny crosses of red, amber and green. Sales of walking sticks, torches and batteries rocketed, as even collisions between pedestrians were common.

My grandmother was now in the flat and in the basement with us. The part of Warsaw where she had been living had been bombed out and cleared, and she had come to Auntie Krysia for shelter. I know no details of how all that happened, but I do know that she presented us with an enormous problem. My grandmother was Russian and spoke very patchy, heavily-accented Polish. To most Poles at that time, anyone who spoke Polish badly had to be Jewish; certainly it was too dangerous to take risks in the matter. So now Auntie Krysia was responsible for a child who had to keep her eyes cast down and a woman who had to keep her mouth shut.

I must tell you that throughout the years of the war, not only did I not know that I was Jewish, but I only had a sketchy idea of what all the fuss and bother was about. I didn't understand that it was a religion. Pola had always made it sound like a tragic condition which could be relieved by baptism. She took me to church and taught me how to cross myself and say all the prayers that a small child should know. I had not been baptised because of the war, of course. There had not been time. There was never the least hint that I might be one of the accursed tribe. She taught me that small Jewish children went to hell when they died. "Were it not for the Jews" she added "Poland would not have been suffering in the first place. If nothing else the Germans were doing one good job. When they'd won the war, at least for that Poland would be grateful to them." I listened and felt quite superior that I was Polish and untainted.

For Pola, Jews were the scourge of Satan. Why she took such care to ensure that this small specimen should survive despite all the Germans' efforts, I cannot explain. When I was with her, she took me to Mass and instructed me. When the war was over, she prepared me for baptism and confirmation. She stitched the beautiful white dress herself and listened to me gabble incomprehensible Latin until I was word-perfect. This was to be her ultimate reward for the risks and the danger.

There were many Poles who knowingly helped to hide Jews and who fed them and helped them to escape. Pola herself was one. The Countess and her daughter were not, but since they both spoke Russian they accepted my grandmother for what she said she was, an unfortunate Russian lady.

In the evening, after the potatoes and sour milk, Auntie Krysia and my grandmother sang Russian songs, to the Countess's great pleasure. Auntie Krysia had a strong, pleasing voice. I learned all the melodies and the odd phrase of the lyrics stuck in my mind.

The flat lost much of its furniture. Maciej's room was now empty of its wonderful toys. I spent a lot of time there, since now there were three of us sleeping in one tiny room; I imagine Auntie Krysia was grateful whenever I was invited to play with Maciej.

I suppose it must have been the lure of the fires that finally made me disobey the strict instructions never to go to the window. As I looked, something whistled past my head, burning my hair. The bullet-hole left a brown mark on the wall behind me but was so small I hoped nobody would see it. I tried to cover my burnt hair. I was afraid of Auntie Krysia's anger when she saw how disobedient I had been. Nothing prepared me for her hysterical tears. The lecture, when it came, was given by the Countess, who made me stand in a corner with my hands behind my back for what seemed like hours. It must have been the most powerful punishment she knew from her own childhood. Now it makes me smile to think of a small girl standing like a dunce in a corner, with her hair and the top of her ear singed by a bullet, while Warsaw burned.

7

London 1943—Judith

I had two Aunts—Queenie and Miriam. I also had an Uncle
Bay, but we never saw him. There had been a big argument
between him, my mother and Auntie Queenie. Apparently it was
something to do with money: he wanted it, they said they'd given
him enough, and in the end he threatened to go away and never
speak to them again. And that's just what he did.

That was a shame because my cousin Brian (Bay's son) didn't
come to play any more. Before that we used to have good games:
pirates and gangsters. The most exciting was called 'The Death
Chair'. I got strapped into a small wicker chair and Brian would
push it down the stairs with me in it. I felt the bumps on each step
and it finally came to a stop on the first landing. My screams were
a mixture of joy, excitement and pure terror.

One day a cat appeared in our garden. It didn't seem to have an
owner, so we brought it in and offered it a few drops of milk in a
saucer. By the end of the week my mother was boiling up bits of

stale fish that she'd bought from MacFisheries just before closing time. It was agreed that the cat could stay.

When Brian noticed that the cat had remarkable eyes—one green and one blue—he brought a friend, Richard, who didn't believe it was true. The boys agreed that the eyes were in fact different and gleefully told me that the cat was probably blind. They played with it for a few minutes but at the first scratch they lost interest and disappeared into my bedroom. I stayed downstairs, chasing the cat under the table, trying to lift it on to my knee.

Brian and Richard were acting out a scene involving gangsters and the police. I didn't know what this meant but they said they needed an extra character. My golliwog, called Oggy, seemed to be the best candidate. Most four year olds had a teddybear but Oggy was the cuddly toy I adored. He shared my bed and I always ran upstairs to get him when we were rushing into the air raid shelter.

Brian liked the golliwog's face and clothes. He was trying to take off his striped trousers and waistcoat when Richard, wanting to get on with the game, started to pull one of the legs. Brian held on tightly to the other leg and both boys yanked and heaved until one of them fell over. The sound of ripping fabric made them drop the golliwog on to the floor. When I saw Oggy, ripped up the middle, stuffing oozing out in lumps, I began to shake and shout. I was crying big wet bubbles of tears. I picked up the golliwog and tried to push the bits of his inside back. The trousers were torn and the buttons were hanging off the velvet waistcoat. My mother was searching on the floor for Oggy's mouth: the yellow smile had come unstuck and was lying on the carpet with a pile of kapok stuffing. He was taken to hospital and brought back a few days later. I did notice that his legs were slightly thinner and there were neat stitches up the inside of his trousers.

Gollywogs in the past—and now: A Golliwog was a black fictional character in 19th century children's books. It was reproduced as a type of rag doll and was popular in the UK and Australia until the 1970s, with companies like Robertsons featuring it on jam labels and offering free Golly badges to customers. The doll was characterised by black skin, eyes rimmed in white, clown lips and frizzy hair. The image of the doll has become the subject of controversy. No longer an innocuous toy, its depiction of African people is understandably now considered racist, especially due to the pejorative term 'wog'.

Golliwogs were banned by the Nazis in 1934 on the grounds that they were inappropriate toys for young German children. The fear was that the supremely non-Aryan black face was so attractive that it would make it harder to teach the young to wash!

Warsaw. Wartime—Marysia

Our block of flats was on fire and there was a constant banging at the doors, warning us to leave. The lights flickered and went out, and by the glow of a candle Auntie Krysia gave us our bundles which had been waiting for this moment. She strapped a rolled blanket to my back and told me that I was never to take off my coat, because it might get stolen and that I must hang on to her belt so we wouldn't get separated. Grandmother complained that her bundles were too heavy. There wasn't time to repack or reorganize. Maciej and his mother were waiting in the hall and he too had a bundle on his back. I picked up my rag doll and Auntie Krysia snatched it away. "That's stupid" she snapped. "You can be carrying more food instead of that rubbish." She threw the doll into the empty room. We all ran down the stairs.

Everything in the street was burning. It is difficult to describe what a burning city looks like. I didn't understand that buildings could fall down or that smoke could choke you. Memories of what happened have become overlaid with the understanding, which came later, of what could have happened. I do remember terror, so strong and fierce that the taste of it is sometimes still in my mouth. But I no longer know how well I understood what there was to be afraid of. Panic is catching and it swept through the cellars and through the streets. The soldier in uniform represented the devil, and Pola had taught me to cross myself whenever I saw one. Nobody has to be taught to fear rats. For the rest, I think I probably caught Auntie Krysia's fear, and trembled when she trembled.

We were in another cellar. Auntie Krysia and I shared a chaise longue. Sometimes my grandmother sat on it. We guarded it.

I walked down a street with Auntie Krysia. The sun was shining and there was rubble under our feet. Auntie Krysia looked very pretty. When we reached our block of flats I saw how tall and deserted it looked. There were broken windows everywhere. Auntie Krysia walked nonchalently up to the two soldiers standing at the gate. She spoke to them in German and they nodded and shrugged. She told me to stay and play next to the kind soldiers and to be good. I saw her run into the empty building and I played on the pavement with stones, as I had been told to do. Why these soldiers should be trusted, I didn't understand. Pola's Hansi had been gentle but he hadn't carried a big gun. The answer must lie in smiling, playing and being good so I smiled, played and waited.

Auntie Krysia came out of the building carrying the large jar of goose fat. The soldiers laughed and we walked away.

We lived in this new cellar for what seemed a long time; it felt like several weeks, through it may have been just days. I remember the smell, the darkness and the precious chaise longue. When we were finally smoked out of there, the door opened and a German with gun and helmet told us to get out. German soldiers had a way of barking their orders that left you in no doubt as to what they wanted you to do. With their greatcoats, guns and helmets they always looked enormous, much bigger than ordinary grown-ups. Once more we walked with our bundles through burning streets at night.

I don't remember how or why we found ourselves in the second cellar. I don't think I ever saw the Countess or Maciej and his mother again. I remember being small, at the level of people's hands and never looking up to see their faces. I remember being tired, hungry, cold and afraid, but above all never talking or crying about it. The smell of burning houses, the sky bright with lights to help the bombers find their targets, the fear of being separated and left behind are all jumbled together. Yet there were some unexpected and cherished pleasures: a man giving me a white box containing a lamb made out of sugar, which I ate a tiny piece at a time, to make it last. Playing snowballs when I was with Pola. Being put in a bath with warm water in it and being afraid that so much extravagance would be found out and punished. At the same time there was always the horror of being filthy. The fear of soldiers. Screaming in the streets. Rats. And above all the fear of being separated and left behind.

The memories are sharp and jagged, even though they are disconnected. There are vivid images of a shoe that hurt and a hat that Auntie Krysia wore. Strangest of all is that I can recall thoughts: I know exactly where I was standing and what I was thinking when the bullet went through my hair and when my friend was shot in the stomach. What I cannot remember in every case is the sequence of events, names and above all faces.

What I Now Know

Gold: When I was leaving the burning flat I had no idea of the reason I was told never to take off my coat. I found out later that Auntie Krysia had sewn gold pieces into the hem.

Auntie Krysia told me many years later that at that time bread and fat were more valuable than gold. You couldn't buy food with gold any more and she couldn't bear the thought of leaving a whole jar of good fat in the empty building, so she risked both our lives to retrieve it.

8

London 1943/44 —Judith

There was a synagogue at the end of our road in Cricklewood.
For some reason we never went there. My father was a member of
another one in Brondesbury and my mother seemed to prefer one
much further away, in Lauderdale Road. It was called the Spanish
and Portuguese and I expect we went there because my mother
was born in Lisbon. When she got married to my father, they
were not allowed to have the ceremony there because he wasn't
Spanish or Portuguese. After that they didn't seem to mind him
coming, because a few years later they seemed to have forgotten
about their rules and allowed him to become a member.

So that's where we went on Saturday mornings. I had a coat with
a velvet collar and I think I kept it on all the time, as it was cold
inside the large building. The singing and prayers went on too
long. I liked to listen to the choir but when I got bored I would
half close my eyes and look up at the lamps hanging from the
ceiling. There were coloured glass windows and if I tilted my head

I could look through my eyelashes and make patterns of light that seemed like cobwebs in shimmering colours.

If I was wearing a new coat my cousins would lean over and whisper 'Consaloo' to me. I never knew what this meant. They were from the Spanish/Portuguese side of the family and I later found out that the words were Con Salud, meaning 'with health'. I could never understand why a coat or dress should come 'with health'—I expected buttons and pockets.

Because of the bombings in London, many people wanted to escape to places where there weren't so many German planes. It was decided that we should go and stay at a farm in Scotland for a while. My father couldn't leave London where he went to his office every day, so David and I travelled with Mummy to a place called Kircoobrie. They told me it was spelt Kirkudbright. Apparently it wasn't bright at all and the farmhouse where we'd planned to stay for a month was horrid.

So we all set off again by train, with our little suitcases and sandwiches packed in greaseproof paper. This time we were going to stay with relatives in the North East of England. We arrived at the station at Newcastle and went on to the house in Barnes View, Sunderland. There was a long drive to the front door and we were greeted by our cousins Mimi, Lionel and their son Harold who was a few years older than David.

Mimi welcomed us with big hugs and smiles. She told us not to worry about food (we had brought our emergency ration books with us). The house wasn't so big, but they made room for all of us to stay. What did we do with ourselves all those weeks, without any of our toys? I know we weren't allowed to go on the beach because it was 'restricted'. We also ate a lot of fish. We shared our rations and talked about the Doodlebugs, the V1 bombs that were raining down on London. The planes—with no pilots—were powered by petrol and when it was used up, we could hear the noise of the engine as it cut out. That was the moment that made people so scared, for it was then that the bombs fell to the ground.

At the Sunderland synagogue there was an event one weekend where they had a raffle. One of the prizes was a lemon and the person who won it was jumping up and down. I couldn't imagine why a lemon would be so exciting—probably because I had never seen one. Mummy did remember what to do with them. Apparently you squeezed a lemon over pancakes and then sprinkled over some sugar. After about a month it was decided that we should go home. The family had been so warm and friendly—especially Mimi—but we wanted to get back to our house in London. Maybe it was because there seemed to be no sign of the rocket bombs stopping, that Mummy decided we should all be together and not leave Daddy on his own.

We were so glad to see him again. We asked him what he had been doing while we were 'up North' as he called it. He reeled off names of cities I didn't know about and told us that Norwich, Canterbury and York had all been bombed while Oxford was spared. Of course I never understood any of this. David and I played, and quarrelled, laughed and poked each other, and ran in from the garden when we were called for supper.

What I Now Know

The bombing: It was believed that Oxford had not been bombed because Hitler wanted to make it his capital if he ever conquered Britain. In early January 1944 the Little Blitz began. It was the Luftwaffe's last atack on London. The raids ended in April, leaving a trail of destruction and death that made Londoners consider leaving.

The risks we faced, the fear of being overrun by German troops, the nightly casualties caused by the endless bombing raids—all this was hidden from me and David. In June 1944, in retaliation for British saturation bombing of major German cities, a final vicious assault began on the capital. Nine thousand people were killed by the V1 's 'vengeance weapons' or ' Vergettungswaffen'.

Outside Warsaw—wartime—Marysia

There is another road and another column of people and more soldiers with bayonets at the side of the road. The pack on my back is very heavy and my grandmother is finding it difficult to walk. There are abandoned packs and suitcases everywhere and my aunt pleads with my grandmother not to give up. She always addresses her very politely, in the third person. She tells her that if she throws away the food and the blanket there'll be no point in walking on anyway.

I know that we have been caught, though I don't know what that means. We are being taken to a transport but I don't know what that means either. The walking is endless.

We are at a railway station and we wait, sitting on our parcels and packets. It is a relief.

The train is very crowded. It is a railway wagon with wooden seats and windows that will not open. People are standing on the seats and between the seats. There is a soldier at each end of the wagon. Auntie Krysia is talking to one of the soldiers. She is laughing. She gives him a watch from her wrist and some pieces of gold. He pushes people to one side so that my grandmother, Auntie Krysia and I are near the door. The people resent being pushed. There is no room. They look at us with fear and with hatred, covertly, but I can see those secret expressions because from my height I can see under their lowered lids. They turn from us. They make way.

When the train slows down Auntie Krysia opens the door and throws me from the train. My bundles follow. I fall on to grass. I know that she has finally got rid of me, and all the whispered, desperate conversations with Pola come back to me. It's too dangerous to look after me... I've been disobedient...I looked up....I wanted to take my doll with me... I dragged my feet...I've been 'recognized' and Auntie Krysia has had to throw me away...

The fall has not hurt me, but fear has left me unable to move. Then I see the train come to a momentary halt before a bridge and Auntie Krysia and grandmother jump out. They run along the ditch and push me down. Auntie Krysia lies on top of me. I hear the train moving away and I hear shouting. There are shots, but the train moves on and we are left in the ditch, with a bridge in front of us and fields all around and silence.

What I Now Know

Leaving the train: At the time I had no idea if we were being singled out for some favour or for quick death, but I sensed that for those on the train to be near us was not safe.

It is likely, though not certain, that the destination of the train was Treblinka. The extermination camp was situated in a forest N.E. of Warsaw.

9

What did I know of the war and the meaning of all the restrictions? I had no understanding of Germans, the Luftwaffe, or Bomber Commmand. I had heard the names Winston Churchill and Hitler on the radio, leaving no doubt who was good and who was bad.

We rarely travelled around the country. The only time I had left my home in Cricklewood was to go up north. I remember the train journey there. Somehow we had managed to buy some cherries (it must have been summer). I sat looking out of the window as the countryside rolled past, popping the cherries into my mouth, one at a time, until the bag was empty. A few minutes later there was a horrible lurching in my stomach and I was sick all over my clothes, the train seat and the floor.

My parents used to talk of holidays on the South coast, specially Eastbourne, the town where they met. They told us about the donkey rides along the beach and the piers ablaze with coloured lights in the evenings. I never quite understood what went on inside, but it was something to do with slot machines.

My mother spent her time queueing. When she went to Walsmans the kosher butcher in Cricklewood Broadway she would be handed a brown paper parcel in return for the ration book coupons. She waited to open the package till she got home. Perhaps she wasn't excited like I would have been, opening a present. Maybe she already knew it would be a disappointment. I heard people say 'you get what you get. There's no point complaining.'

Sometimes there would be breasts of lamb, cut into pieces, and that meant we would have lamb and barley stew for supper. It seemed to be bubbling on the stove for hours and when it came out of the pot you had to blow on it. The first fatty mouthful was hot and deliciously soft. It was sometimes hard to find the bits of meat. At other times, there would just be a pile of bones and a few sausages. I think my mother was good at magic because the bones were turned into soup with carrots and beans and that tasted good too. One time we had some kind of meat in a dark thick gravy. It tasted strong and was rubbery in my mouth. I found out later that it was ox heart.

What I Now Know

Travel and holidays: Because the ports were in danger, the coastal towns, previously used by holidaymakers, were virtually shut down. The piers—long wooden or metal structures which had been alive with shows and amusement arcades—were now taken over by the Navy. Sea fronts were quiet and desolate; parks were closed. The beaches were sealed off by concrete barriers and the sandy coastline was probably mined.

Travelling around the countryside was made more difficult as station nameboards had been removed and signposts on the roads were turned in the wrong direction. All this was to confuse any possible invading army.

Lowicze, Central Poland—Wartime—Marysia

Being thrown from a train must have briefly knocked out my memory. We weren't hurt but the walk that followed remains a blank in my mind. All I knew was that we were walking to a nearby town called Lowicze. Yet the train, the people, the soldier, the conviction that I was being thrown out because Auntie Krysia was angry with me—all that stayed with me. There was no Pola to save me. I didn't have a chance to cling on. Then there was the relief of seeing my aunt, followed by the horror of being stifled as she lay on top of me and would not move. Then the quiet as we sat in the ditch, at the bottom of the bank with the railway line just above us. There was no time for comforting or explanations.

I remember Lowicze. We lived in a single room in a flat belonging to two sisters who looked on us with loathing. A German officer in high polished boots came to call. The sisters brought something to drink in tiny cups and left the room. They spat at the door after they had closed it and then they spat at me. I sat at the foot of the closed door and heard laughter on the other side.

Auntie Krysia, blonde and beautiful, had stopped a German officer in Lowicze and had asked for his protection, spinning some fantastic story about losing her home, her husband and her way! She must have used up a lifetime's supply of courage to do this, but she had very little to lose. We could not have survived in open country, and nobody would have taken us in, not even for gold. The native population of Poland had learnt the German rules very well by this time, as well as the penalties for breaking them. Three stray women were too dangerous to shelter. The German officer had swallowed Auntie Krysia's story and offered us his protection. He billeted us on the sisters, who must have assumed they were having to put up the worst kind of collaborator and camp follower. Auntie Krysia was afraid of them. She was terrified of the Gestapo officer, who called regularly in his beautiful pressed clothes. He bowed low over her hand. He always asked if we were being given enough to eat. Auntie Krysia smiled at the sisters and told him of their generosity and kindness. I wriggled with indignation, because I was always hungry.

The sisters made shoes out of rope and old cloth, and soon we were making ourselves useful. Auntie Krysia sat in silence winding the rope to make up the soles and I sat next to her, holding the soles steady as she sewed them. Her fingers hurt. My grandmother matched the cloth for the uppers so that the finished shoes looked as much like a pair as possible. Few words were ever exchanged.

"Cotton"
"Scissors"
"More rope".

I tried to smile at them, but they ignored me. I simpered, dropping little curtsies whenever one of the sisters came into the room, showing off all the beautiful little manners that I had been taught would charm the adult population into submission. They refused to be manipulated. Auntie Krysia kept me to heel and would not permit any show of resentment on my part. She helped them sew ropes into soles until her fingers bled, and I ran little errands and helped in every way with a pretty smile. If I failed in any detail, Auntie Krysia reminded me with a sharp pinch.

Then—again for reasons I cannot remember—we left Lowicze and went to a small village where again all three of us lived in one room. The German officer took us there and billeted us, but thereafter his visits were infrequent. Our very reluctant hosts took out their spite on us in small but effective ways. They decided to keep their pig outside our window all summer, so that the stench and the noise would force us to keep our window closed all the time. Summers in Poland are very hot. In the winter we were kept well away from the kitchen stove. There was a bench near the door where we were supposed to sit while the family warmed their backs. They preferred us to stay in our room where they didn't have to look at us.

We must have been in that village for about a year, and for part of that time Pola was there too, though she did not stay in the same house. How she came and why she went I can't remember, but while she was there I was happy. I went into the fields with her when it was time to pick potatoes. My nimble fingers picked the small potatoes the row of advancing women left behind. There was gossip. I learnt to relieve myself standing up, by just straddling my legs and lifting my skirt up a little. Pola found me a heavy striped peasant skirt which came to my ankles and made me feel that I belonged to the group of children who slowly began to accept me as one of them and let me play with them. I wiped my nose on my sleeve or on the hem of my skirt, and washed my hands and feet in the communal tub just inside the front door. Even so, I was not allowed to sit near the stove.

The house was long and low. The door led directly into the kitchen, where the huge, welcoming stove stood like an iron whale. It was used for cooking, for warming the room and for heating water. In the winter the family slept around it. There was a fierce grandmother who terrorized the farmer and his wife. They, in their turn, took out their spite on their own children and on us—three extra unwelcome mouths to feed, dumped on them by the hated Germans.

Auntie Krysia bought bacon and anything else that could be had on the black market. This was kept in our room under a floorboard and eaten in haste and secrecy, in tiny quantities. The main meal of the day, however, was included in our rent and every day as this event approached, the tension mounted. The grandmother, in her ballooning skirt and headscarf, guarded the food on the stove. She, too, had secret supplies of pork, apples and potatoes which she was not prepared to share with strangers. She kept her own family strictly rationed. However much rent Auntie Krysia paid her, she was not going to let her into the secret of her forbidden stores. I found out about them, however, because once, when playing, I had discovered her storeroom behind bales of straw in a barn and thereafter had regularly crept in and stolen small quanties of apples and slices of crispy pork.

She decreed that we were to eat in our own room. My grandmother and I went there and waited. Auntie Krysia stood with a bowl, hopefully deep, to be graciously filled for us. Our dinner was always gruel. The grandmother only filled Auntie Krysia's bowl from one of the large pots simmering on the stove. The others remained firmly closed, with sweet odours seeping from beneath their lids. In our bowl there were three small potatoes, sometimes a very small piece of meat, one or two carrots, and barley or oats to thicken it all. There was no seasoning. The meat was always given to me because I was supposed to be growing. Auntie Krysia watched me chew endlessly and swallow. I was the one who worked in the fields. I was the one who warmed the icy bed every night before Auntie Krysia and my grandmother could bear to get in. I felt, with great pride, that I had earned my tiny morsel of meat, however tough and tasteless.

Auntie Krysia spent her days sewing and knitting for the family. She sat by the window, unraveling old jumpers in order to make new ones. She also unpicked collars and jackets, turning them over and sewing them back together with the fresher looking cloth on the outside. My grandmother, short-sighted with poor Polish, unskilled, spoiled all her life by a doting older husband, had little to offer in a house where such idleness was only tolerated in the very, very old. The family made her bread of idleness bitter indeed, and I tried to work harder and be even more of a simpering, obliging little angel to make up for it.

10

London—1944—Judith

My parents started to whisper that 'the air raids had started again' mentioning places I had never been to. I'd heard of the Houses of Parliament, but what was The Treasury or Horse Guards Parade? We were too far away to hear any noise from the bombs that came down on those buildings, but it seems that on one night in January hundreds of aeroplanes dropped fire bombs on the city.

I was just learning to read and saw big words in the newspaper "Paddington Station hit." Every day I walked to my school, St. Helens in Willesden Green. We often saw a newly bombed-out house. We got used to seeing shattered windows and blackout curtains torn by the broken glass.

David was at a school called Westcroft. He didn't talk about the boys there, but he was very excited about some news he had heard. Apparently one of his friends had seen a great silver elephant in the sky. It was in Gladstone Park and was called a barrage balloon. It was fixed to the ground with wire cables and was there, with the anti-aircraft guns, to try to stop the enemy planes.

The silver balloon had been in the sky for a few weeks before David was allowed to go and see it. That was because he was ill. One day he got a sore throat and red spots all over his body. The doctor was called. After much mumbling, with my parents going in and out of his room, it became clear that I should not go in, because he had Scarlet Fever.

After several days I began to post little notes under his door as he couldn't come out, being in something called 'isolation'. Scarlet Fever was very catching and it was only then that I realized how much I missed playing with him. Doctors and nurses seemed to come and go every few days, checking the spots and taking his temperature to see if he was getting better.

Whenever either of us was ill, with measles or mumps, Mummy would bring hot drinks and food up to our rooms. As she climbed the stairs she would sing a song which began: "Rumpity, tumpity, tumpity tump, here comes the galloping major." I felt excited as I heard her footsteps. It stopped me thinking about my itchy skin. I heard the words repeated as she walked up the stairs carrying a tray."Hi Hi get out of the way, here comes the galloping major." When she came into my room she would put down a plate of buttered bread fingers and a few peeled grapes. If you had a sore throat these were things which 'went down easily.'

Around that time, my mother kept disappearing. Not for days and nights, but she stopped coming to fetch me on time from school. I remember her running up to the entrance, panting and apologising. When I asked her where she'd been she wouldn't tell me. One day she came home late in the evening. I could see she had been crying. My father put his arms around her and she started sobbing even louder. All I could hear were the words 'Mother' 'Dead.'

In the next few days I heard arguments and noisy quarrels about something called a will. Where was my grandmother? She could have sorted it out.

What I Now Know

The bombing: After a lull lasting two and a half years, German aircraft, flying in two waves, targeted London again. On the night of 21st January 1944, four hundred enemy planes unleashed bombing that killed 1,500 people and injured 3,000. It was called The Little Blitz.

Most of this was concentrated on the centre of London, in Westminster near the river. Where we lived, six miles away, the hits were largely accidental, so though some houses were certainly destroyed, the damage was mostly shattered windows. Our parents managed to conceal the worries they had and never conveyed a sense of danger to David and me.

The barrage balloons: A number of aircraft used by Nazi Germany during its Blitzkrieg campaigns relied on diving to release bombs accurately. Some even had special sirens fitted to their wings. This increased the noise produced when the planes lost height and struck fear into those on the ground. To counter this low-flying threat, balloons were raised with heavy cables designed to destroy low flying aircraft, forcing them up into the effective range of Anti-Aircraft Defences.

Childhood illnesses: In those days the most serious infectious diseases were scarlet fever, diptheria and typhoid fever. Worst of all was polio which killed or maimed millions of people during the 1940s and 1950s. Treatment with penicillin for scarlet fever was a breakthrough, leaving it a disease that was highly contagious, but not life-threatening.

My memory of buttered bread and peeled grapes brought to my bedside must have been at a later time. They would not have been available then, but were more likely what I ate to ease the sore throat that preceded a long bout of chicken pox a few years later.

Poland—1944—Marysia

It was in that village that I had my first taste of school. It was announced that a teacher was coming and that all the children were to have lessons. This must have been during the summer, because I remember running with bare feet through the grass with my doorstep of bread tucked into my pinafore.

We were arranged in a circle with slates and I sat poised, brimming with excitement and anticipation. I was not at all sure what was meant by school, teacher, learning or lessons, but Auntie Krysia had been delighted, and I was going to be with the other children.

The teacher was old and very serious. He asked if anybody could read and, since nobody else answered, I kept very quiet. I thought I knew how to read, but since none of the big children around me answered I quickly came to the conclusion that one should not speak to a teacher. Or perhaps I couldn't read and something completely different was being asked for. Perhaps what I did when I opened a book wasn't reading at all.

The teacher wrote the letter "A" on a slate and held it up for everybody. Then he pronounced it very slowly. He rubbed out "A" and wrote "B". The performance was repeated right through the alphabet, twice.

"Now", he said. "I'll see how many letters you can remember. When I call out a letter, you write it down." He called out letters at random. Without any thought that I might be showing off or that I might be drawing unfavourable attention to myself, I wrote down the letters. The teacher snatched my slate away. "You knew them before, didn't you? You know all your letters."

"Yes".

"You can read, can't you?" he said accusingly.

"I don't know." I hung my head.

All eyes were on me, sneering. It was not at all clever to know how to read before you had been taught. I had not been given permission to know all these letters. Pola had told me never, never to stand out in any way. I felt that my bladder was going to burst with terror. I was very hot.

The teacher held me by one shoulder and pushed an open book in front of me.

"Can you read that?" he asked.

The print was large. The words were short and simple, or broken up into syllables. The books I had lived with under my table in Warsaw had not looked like that at all. Perhaps there was a difference. Perhaps it was only called 'reading' when the print was large and there were pictures on the page.

"Yes!" I said, with a sigh of relief.

"Read it then!" I read.

"So why didn't you say you could read?" he asked.

"Didn't you hear me? Didn't I make myself clear?"

"Oh, yes" I said. "I didn't know this was called reading. My books don't look like this. The print is very small and there are proper words in my books."

There was a stunned silence. The teacher cuffed me hard on the ear.

"So.We didn't know this was called reading? So this is too simple for our little know-all here. Didn't know that this was called reading, indeed! How old are you?"

"Five, sir." I dipped a curtsy and tried to smile through my tears.

"There's no need for that nonsense. And when did you learn to read?"

Underneath his irritation I sensed admiration. I could, after all, do something that the other children could not do. And that must make me superior in some way, however dangerous the consequences. "I don't know, sir." I said with a little curtsy. I didn't think that could do any harm. It was like crossing yourself in church; the more you did it, the more those around you could see that you were good. "I can't remember when I couldn't, sir. I think I must have been born with it."

I sighed. He laughed. On the way home the other children threw clods of earth at me. The next time we had a class I confessed at once that I knew my numbers up to one hundred.

The teacher set me some small addition sums on my slate and I was happy when I couldn't get them right. The journey back home would not be such a trial.

11

London—1944/45—Judith

When I went on the bus I could hear people talking all around me—and though I had no knowledge of accents, I could distinguish the voices of the different groups who lived near Cricklewood.

There were the Irish who mainly shared crowded flats in Kilburn. The English lived in larger houses with a drive, bay windows and well tended back gardens.

It was some time before I discovered this and I learned it from eavesdropping on the conversations on the bus.

Of course at the age of five I had little idea of what religion meant. At the end of our road was a church, St. Gabriel's, which was almost opposite the synagogue. From that I might have assumed there were an equal number of Christians and Jews. My arithmetic was not good enough to work out that although we knew many Jewish families, there must have been far more neighbours who were known as 'C of E'.

We lived in an area that was probably established in the 19th century by a family who originated in Devon. The street names all reflected that. Of course we had no car—no-one did at that time—so we walked to the library, the shops and the underground station. I had never been to the real towns but I was quite familiar with Sidmouth Rd, Dawlish Rd, Teignmouth Rd, Dartmouth Rd, Exeter Rd and Lydford Rd. My own street was a cause for amusement. Walm Lane (pronounced 'warm') joined Cricklewood to Willesden and years later when I was walking home with friends who came from further away, they would often ask me 'are we getting 'warmer'?'

There was simply no mention of the fact that we were Jewish or any hint that we didn't belong there. Both my parents spoke perfect English, were educated at university in London and Cambridge and didn't consider themselves in any way foreigners.

Something changed when new people arrived in the country with a different way of speaking. You would hear loud voices on the buses, talking in a German accent. People standing in a queue for food would push their way to the front, not understanding the English system of waiting your turn. The words 'Black Market' were spoken in a sneering tone by my parents. I could only make out that some people were trying to obtain more than their fair share of the rations.

My grandfather in Mapesbury Road had an Austrian maid called Maria. She seemed to be in charge of everything. I never spoke to her. She had a sharp voice and seemed to dominate the household. She was not unkind in any way I could see. There were whispers that she was a 'German sympathiser.' I got confused with these conversations because there was also talk of the German refugees buying goods on the Black Market and paying for 'illegally obtained delicacies'. None of this made sense to me as I couldn't understand any of these words.

Life continued as normal. I got on the No 16 bus and heard the conductor call 'Crown Cricklewood' when it arrived at the end of The Broadway. The Crown was one of a dozen pubs to be found between my home area and the bustling Kilburn High Road. I didn't know it was a place to buy beer, and thought it was a palace with its massive pillars and terracotta brickwork.

I went with my mother to have my teeth checked by a dentist in Shoot-up-Hill.

I have written proof of this! When I was about five or six I wrote letters to the fairies who would leave presents in the night, in exchange for a tooth that had fallen out.

Dear Fairies
My tooth came out. I told Oggy about it.
Love from Judith and Oggy

Dear Fairies
David's tooth is at Mr. Birkhahn's house. Please put David's present under his pillow.
Love from Judith.

What I Now Know

The Jewish refugees: By 1938 there were about 10,000 Jewish refugees in Britain, the vast majority of them from Germany. After the Anschluss refugees from Austria and Germany could no longer simply arrive at British ports, to be welcomed by sympathetic immigration officers. Would-be refugees had to obtain prior approval abroad before they could enter. By 1939 there were about 78,000 in Britain. After that date, in order to get a visa they needed to have a deposit of £50 (today's equivalent would be nearly £3,000) but as it was illegal to have foreign currency in Germany at that time, this route would have been almost impossible. The problem was solved when the Jewish community offered to provide assistance with housing, education and job training, thus releasing the Government from any financial responsibilities.

For women, the only way was to come as a domestic. Most of them came from well off Viennese families. They were warned to bring warm clothes to deal with the cold of an English house and were put to work from 8 am to 11pm cleaning and scrubbing. They had an hour's break during this long shift and half a day off a week. One young woman complained. The lady of the house replied:"If it's too much for you, I'll send you back to Hitler."

My grandfather's domestic help Maria was a mystery. She was not Jewish. She was employed years before when my grandmother was still alive. Apparently she played a large part in looking after her, and later took over the running of the house. Maria was extremely efficient, with a domineering streak that didn't endear her to my father and mother. How on earth did she come to be working in England for a Jewish family during the war?

Poland—in the village 1945—Marysia

At about this time a new source of fear entered our lives. "The Cossacks are coming." The Cossacks had an insatiable appetite for women and wristwatches. They swept through the village once. All but the oldest and youngest women were hidden in barns and granaries. No story, however horrendous, was kept from the ears of the children. I talked to one Cossack. He had wristwatches all the way up both arms. He liked my smile and my little curtsy and patted me on the head.

Auntie Krysia had a new fear now that the Russians were on their way. We had been billeted on the family by a German officer. So what would this new army do to us once they were quite sure that the Germans had lost the war?

Groups of tired, bedraggled young German soldiers wandered through the village. Nobody touched them. Nobody spoke to them. We stared at them from behind half-closed doors and shutters, unable to comprehend. The sight of an unkempt German army, its weary tatters shambling along roads and across fields in undisciplined groups, was too difficult to accept. It was a miracle, but nobody was prepared to trust it. They would regroup. They were invincible. I had never known anything else. Auntie Krysia was trying to prepare for every possible turn of events.

The peasants did nothing to the Germans and they did nothing to us. However canny they may have been, they were just as overwhelmed by circumstances as we were. Rumours had reached us, but the reality was still a shock. The rumoured advance of the Russians was not looked upon as bringing relief, but as simply one more wave of marauding hordes. On the other hand Auntie Krysia saw the possibility of rescue if only they would come quickly, before our hosts finally accepted that the German army was defeated.

When they did come, it was my grandmother who stood in the middle of the road, clapping her hands and singing the praises of the Red Army in her beautiful Moscow Russian. She was swept off her feet and carried along triumphantly by the soldiers, who could not believe that they had found a real live Russian babushka in the middle of Poland. Auntie Krysia and I followed.

My grandmother was presented to the commanding officer, and that evening Auntie Krysia sang sentimental Russian ballads as the vodka and tears flowed. I was not quite sure what all the fuss was about. I could see that my grandmother was being treated like a queen and that Auntie Krysia was receiving homage. For me, it was just a change of soldiers and I was still being given the same instructions: 'keep your eyes lowered, don't say anything, smile a lot, curtsy, call everybody 'sir', don't answer any questions, don't ask any questions, and don't leave my side.'

We left the village with the Russians, installed in a horse-drawn cart. The column of Russians was endless and they called out to my grandmother and Auntie Krysia, who called back cheerfully. "Laugh" Auntie Krysia hissed at me. "They want you to laugh." I laughed.

We passed groups of German soldiers and the Russians rounded them up like cattle and goaded them into the column with bayonets. I was cold. The young Russian driving our cart noticed and shouted to one of his friends. A group of Germans was stopped, their greatcoats stripped off with scant ceremony and piled on top of us like blankets. The Germans were only boys and I remember feeling sorry for them. They were so frightened and bedraggled. Now that I no longer feared them I could only pity them. I had not known that it was possible to pity Germans, so I cried. Both Auntie Krysia and my grandmother tried to stop me, in case my crying should irritate the Russians, who were drunk with vodka and triumph. A sniveling child can be very irritating indeed. Somehow, the memory of that journey is one of tears, with new fears and old fears all jumbled in a way I could not begin to understand. The cart rumbled on slowly. These new soldiers were friendly, but Auntie Krysia's and my grandmother's tension only increased as the journey progressed. The amount of vodka being consumed was amazing. Auntie Krysia did not know that I was well used to men reeling with vodka and even had a cabaret act for their amusement. I tried to comfort her, but that just made her more nervous.

The commanding officer accompanied us to our flat in Lódz. It was palatial. Somebody was living there and he threw them out, without even letting them pack a suitcase. He brought vodka and food, and made Auntie Krysia a gift of her own home.

So the war was over and I was back in the home I had left as a baby of nine months. There we all lived for a year, until it was time to leave Lódz and Poland, and start a new life.

12

London—1945—Judith

The foggy days of autumn had passed. The winter brought frost and chilblains. I got sores on my feet because I used to toast my toes in front of the electric fire after coming in on a freezing day.

Then came the summer when we spent most of our time outdoors in the garden. In Walm Lane the chickens took up most of the space and I can't ever remember my parents sitting out in deckchairs. At Mapesbury Road there were long loungers, used by my grandfather and Aunt Miriam—probably a relic from the days when grandmother was stroking or just being ill. There was a huge plum tree and the golden yellow plums were the sweetest, most delicious things I have ever eaten. I remember the juice running down my chin and that luscious golden flesh.

We never went to Finchley any more. I have so few memories of my grandmother, who had died: I think of stupid things like the upright deckchairs she had. She used to tell me to keep my fingers out of them because it was easy for them to get squeezed when you were packing them up to take inside when the rain came. But my main memories of summer are of sunshine and playtime in that garden, and my grandmother smiling while I played with my brother. She must have been happy, standing by the trellis with climbing roses, watching David pull me round the grass on a small cart with a handle. I wore a pretty flower-printed dress with a lacy knitted top, all handmade by my mother. She actually made an identical jumper for herself. That must have taken her a while because it was much bigger since she was quite fat and I was a small child.

After we went home on the trolleybus, we'd walk down Walm Lane, into the driveway and go straight through into the kitchen. On the dresser, underneath the cup hooks was the radio which was always switched on. It was tuned to the General Forces Programme.There were comedy shows and Music While you Work, dancy music that got me jumping up and down. Sometimes my parents would say shhhh when it was interrupted for a news item. These were always about bombings; the House of Commons, something important in a place called Hiroshima and finally news of street parties. It seemed that the war had come to an end in Europe. People poured out of their houses to set up tables in the street and bring whatever food they had to share with the neighbours. This didn't happen in Walm Lane. Perhaps it was in places which suffered the worst of the bombings. My parents' relief was never discussed—at least, not in front of me and David.

What I Now Know

The end of the war: Victory in Europe was declared in May 1945 after Hitler committed suicide. It was the culmination of five years of war, which saw nearly 340,000 allied forces evacuated from Dunkirk and the landing of British and American troops on the Normandy beaches in June 1944. This marked the start of a long and costly campaign to liberate north-west Europe from German occupation. World War II finally came to an end after atomic bombs were dropped on Hiroshima and Nagasaki in August 1945.

Music and morale: Music While you Work was a radio programme which played popular music continuously during the day. The even tempo of the non-stop light music helped factory workers to become more productive. For a period a third edition was broadcast in the early hours for night-shift workers.

News of what was happening on the Continent was sparse, apart from what the Government chose to tell the public. For six years it had been important to keep up the morale of the British people, so they could deal with hardship and intermittent bombing. The fear of invasion was at its most intense in 1940. Bad news from campaigns in other countries like Italy and North Africa contributed to disquiet and sometimes pessimism. The Ministry of Information offered soothing mottos, such as Keep Calm and Carry on.

The flat in Lódz—1945/6 Marysia

My father had been a director and owner, together with his family, of a stocking factory. This had been taken over by the Germans, who had continued to run it. They had installed a German manager who had moved into my parents' abandoned flat, so that when we returned, not only was everything there in good order but all their treasures had been added. The greatest treasures were to be found in my room. The Germans had obviously had a little girl of their own, for lined up against the wall was a column of fourteen dolls, some with real hair and eyes that opened and closed, with boxfuls of dolls' clothes, with cots and a real pram with a hood. There was a doll's house which was taller than me. The front came away to reveal rooms on three floors, with a polished staircase, fine chairs with rounded backs and green velvet seats, chandeliers, Persian rugs and real oil paintings on the walls. Next, under the window there was a dappled rocking horse with a red saddle and a long tail. There was a table for me with two small chairs and a miniature tea set. In the wardrobe there were little dresses, which fitted me.

It took a long time for me to start playing with the toys. At first I just stared at them. Sometimes I would stroke the dolls. I stared at the miniature mansion and lifted out one small item of furniture to admire it. I never believed that all these wonders could be meant for me, so I began to give them away.

In Poland blocks of flats are built round a courtyard which you enter through an archway large enough to take a carriage at least, sometimes even bigger. In our courtyard the children gathered to play. I was small, a newcomer, did not speak as they did and behaved like a stunted grown-up. The children certainly did not welcome me in their games. At most I was allowed to stand in a corner and watch. Then, one day, I came down with a doll and discovered that I had purchasing power: if I gave a toy, I was allowed to play. I tried to eke out my capital as best I could, but my room became rapidly depleted and I was relegated to my corner again. Auntie Krysia did not discover what I had done for a while, but when she did she was aghast. She called the children swine and me a little fool, as much for wanting to play with them as for giving them my toys. She told me that I must never give away my things without gaining some advantage. Since I wanted to be included in the children's games more than I wanted the toys, it seemed to me that the bargain was weighted in my favour, but she wouldn't see it from my point of view. She continued to scold. She had never before been angry with me for that sort of reason. There was no problem of safety or of food, so I could not understand why she should be so upset. It took me a long time to understand why any grown-up should be cross with me for what I considered 'trivial' reasons.

Auntie Krysia had to go out to work, because the law required it. We had a lodger in my father's study, because there had to be a minimum number of people in a flat. Pola came back to live with us. My happiness was complete.

What I Now Know

The dresses in the cupboard: The 'lodger' was billeted on us, probably by the Russians. He was an artist and in lieu of rent painted a portrait of me, wearing one of the dresses left behind by the little girl who had lived there previously. It shows me in a pink dress with small blue bows and a huge blue ribbon in my hair. We still have this picture in our family today.

13

It turned out that we had some family in America. These were not my Spanish and Portuguese relations, but cousins of my father. He told me that his family originally came from Germany, and the ones who fled to America must have escaped before the war started. My father had come much earlier. He must have done because he went to a school in Hackney, East London, called The Grocer's School. I don't think he was ever training to be a grocer. He turned out to be a Patent Agent. When people asked me what that meant I replied that it was something to do with inventions.

My father didn't talk about his work. I imagine people didn't do much inventing during the war, so he had time to read instead of going to the office. He always had his nose in a book. By the way, he had a very big curved nose which he claimed was the result of having a fall and breaking it when he was young. I'm not sure this is true because I know lots of people with big noses who haven't had a fall. Anyway, he and his nose walked once a week to Willesden library. He would come back with a dozen books and read through most of them before returning them the following week.

Reading and teaching us to read was very important for my father. That was the serious side of him. He was also a joker, telling stories which weren't true. One day he went out and sat on a nearby bench. He was approached by a young man selling encyclopaedias. My father brushed him off by saying: 'I'm afraid I can't read so they won't be any use to me.' The salesman went on and a few minutes later knocked on the front door of our house. My mother let him in and listened while he explained that the children would benefit from having a set of the reference books. At that moment my father appeared. The salesman looked from him to the rest of the family, taking in the bookshelves on the wall. He then left hurriedly. After he had gone my father had some explaining to do.

Thinking about all this has made me forget what I started to write about: the family in America. One day, out of the blue, a parcel arrived from the USA. It was enormous. Inside was a doll for me. I had never seen a doll before; there simply weren't any in the shops. This one had eyes with long eyelashes and a sticky out dress with layers of petticoats. You could take off the shoes and plait the hair, fixing it with ribbons. My parents were speechless. I took the doll upstairs and put it on my bed, next to Oggy. But I never talked to it. And it wasn't cuddly like he was.

A few weeks later another parcel arrived. This one contained food and my parents were delighted to see tins and packets as they unwrapped the brown paper. When they saw what was inside their faces fell. There were tins of meat and a piece of ham. No doubt the Americans thought we were starving and would eat anything, but they may not have known that we kept kosher so that what they sent was a big mistake. I expect my parents gave it all to Beatis, but they didn't stop grumbling about it for days. I think this was the first time I had an inkling of 'keeping kosher'. The food ration in Britain included bacon and Jews were allowed to get extra coupons to buy something else. But apart from that I knew nothing of the intricacies of the laws in the Bible telling us what was permitted and what we were never to touch.

Apart from the rationing which showed no signs of stopping, life began to get more exciting. Auntie Queenie always took us to a Christmas show: the Bertram Mills Circus at Olympia. We had to get there early to see all the animals in the stalls before the performance began. I can still smell the sawdust on the ground as we walked from one to another. There were lions, tigers and a couple of brown bears who rode scooters. Six elephants were trained to walk along with their front legs on the backs of the ones in front of them. The programme also included less dangerous creatures like chimpanzees and horses. When the show started I could hardly contain myself. We had to sit through a certain amount of acrobats and juggling, but when the first lion appeared it was breathtaking. Even though the trainers looked so confident, we all realized how dangerous it was, parading wild animals around the inside of a tent filled with hundreds of children.

Birthdays were getting better too. Parties began again and it was the fashion to go in 'fancy dress'. I have no recollection of what anyone else wore. Did they have a mother who designed and executed brilliant costumes? Mummy made me and David a couple of spectacular outfits: we arrived at a party dressed as Sir Walter Raleigh and Queen Elizabeth. David had a sword, brocade breeches, a crisp white ruffle around his neck and a brooch studded with emeralds. I had a tiny crown on my head and my long gown was made of crimson velvet and beige satin. Where did all this finery come from?

What I Now Know

The food ration: Bacon was not included in the meat ration. It was considered an absolutely necessary part of anyone's diet so came in a category of its own. Vegetarians, Jews and Muslims were allowed to use their ham or bacon allowance on cheese instead. Food rationing continued in Britain till well after the war, 1954, while it was discontinued in Germany in 1950.

My father's work: My father was one of two patent agents working together. They had two or three big clients and his work was concerned with technical chemical inventions. His partner dealt with the engineering side. It was unlikely that there was no work during the war, but perhaps my father spent less time at the office than usual, allowing him to read the many books that interested him. Clearly, I had the mistaken impression that he sat at home reading all day!

The Circus: What went on in the Grand Hall at Olympia is now seen as a display of cruelty to animals. At that time it was the most exciting show ever devised for children and adults. No-one thought that animals were being harmed by the discipline they were put through; we were too preoccupied at the risks taken by the trainers and handlers.

Perhaps when stories of real and immense cruelty to human beings were beginning to emerge from Europe, thoughts about performing animals came low on the list of concerns.

The fancy dress costumes: I never asked at the time, but I assume the fabrics were pieces of old curtains. After my grandfather died, the house in Mapesbury Road was sold so they may have come from there. The crown and jewels were probably acquired at a street market.

Lódz. 1946—Marysia

I had piano lessons. I had dancing lessons. In the morning I went to a little school where nobody seemed to mind that I could read and even write a little. My grandmother bought me ice-creams wedged in little wafer shells.

My Aunt Barbara, my father's sister, who was married to a French diplomat and lived in Peru, sent precious exit papers and tickets which would allow her mother to join her. My grandmother refused to leave by herself. She loved Auntie Krysia as a daughter and they had been through too much together to be separated now. She dug her heels in. Letters came and went. Aunt Barbara protested that she could not stretch her husband's diplomatic privileges to incude two more people. Auntie Krysia was young and would forge a good life for herself in Poland. Aunt Barbara could not take on responsibility for another adult and child whose maintenance would inevitably fall on her shoulders. My grandmother understood her point of view and the problems that might arise. Without us, however, she was not going anywhere.

All the discussions and arguments took place in front of me. I suppose that at this stage, having lived through every horror, it did not occur to anyone that anything might be unsuitable for me to hear or that I couldn't take part in any discussion, merely because I was six. My Aunt Barbara's handwriting was large and spidery, sprawling irregularly across blue air-mail paper. She thanked Auntie Krysia for all the care she had taken of her mother, but pointed out that it was for her mother to repay any debt of gratitude that she might feel and that she herself should not be asked to do the impossible in order to discharge these debts. She hoped that later she would be able to help us in some way, but meanwhile, more than anything else, she wanted to see her mother, and it was Auntie Krysia's duty to persuade her to go.

I did not want my grandmother to go and said so most firmly. It was at this time, during the complications over Aunt Barbara and my grandmother, that Auntie Krysia told me that she was, after all, my mother. She told me all the reasons why she had become my Auntie Krysia and that, now the war was won, it was safe for me to call her 'Mummy' again. She explained it very carefully, telling me how hard it had been to be called 'Auntie' by her own little girl and how happy we would be now that she didn't have to pretend any more.

At first I didn't believe her. Being an orphan was quite special, and Pola had always described me as an orphan; I didn't want to lose my importance. Moreover, if Auntie Krysia was my Mother, she must be more important than Pola, and that was something I could not accept at all. Auntie Krysia had always spoiled me more than Pola. She was more tender. She hugged and kissed me more. But Pola made me feel safer and I loved Pola much, much more.

I suppose I must have been pleased about it in some ways. I know that for a long, long time I found it very difficult to call Auntie Krysia 'Mummy' and that every time I stumbled over the unfamiliar word she was upset. Yet every time we met somebody new, I introduced her with enormous pride.

Meeting new people was something that happened to me every time we walked down the street. Few children had survived. I was stroked and petted, given sweets. My Mother was asked how she had saved me. Women cried over me.

When I say few children, I mean few Jewish children. This was the second blow I received at this time. Pola told me that I was one of those poor unfortunate children destined never to go to heaven. She, however, planned to save me. I was to be prepared for baptism and confirmation together, and Pola supervised my instruction. She told me that I must keep it a great secret when she took me to the priest. She drummed incomprehensible Latin into me, and sweetened the whole process by showing me, every now and again, the beautiful white dress she was sewing for me.

She also drummed into me that she was much more my mother than Auntie Krysia. If I stayed with this new mother, not only would she tear me away from Pola, but she would take me to a place where they spoke a strange language I would never understand, and after it was all over and I was dead I would go to hell. Since my Mother was at work all day, Pola had plenty of time to put her case across. She did not rest. I had set pieces to learn by heart every day. Ever bleaker pictures of hell were brandished before me whenever I stumbled over a word or looked longingly out of the window. The prospect of being torn from Pola by this rediscovered Mother and taken away before the seal of certainty could be set on my salvation made me cry at night. Pola heard me crying, but did nothing to remove the cause of my terror. We became fellow conspirators, bent on foiling my Mother's horrible plans for me.

Exhausted by the years of war, anaemic, run-down and working in an office where her few skills were stretched to breaking-point, my Mother would come home and collapse into bed. I hardly ever saw her. Often I heard bitter rows between her and Pola. She would not allow me to visit Pola's family in the country, for she was terrified that, if she ever let me go, Pola would never bring me back. Pola told me to whine and plead.

My grandmother, sweet but ineffectual, was afraid that Pola might approach the authorities and do something to stop us leaving. She smiled at Pola and gave her presents which were taken as of right.

"She owes me more than that!" Pola said to me. "After all I did for you, she owes me a great deal more than that."

At last Aunt Barbara sent the extra tickets and we were set to go. My Mother swore us to secrecy.

She sold everything in the flat and bought herself a fur jacket and some gold. The proceeds of all our possessions were smelted down into a gold powder compact. We were not allowed to take anything of value with us so the powder compact was the way my Mother smuggled out what was left of our worldly goods, to fund our new life.

She told Pola that she was selling her beautiful silver and china because we did not have enough to live on. Pola did not believe her. She plied me with questions whenever we were alone, but by this time I was too much of an expert to give anything away. Each of them had sworn me to secrecy, so there was a balance of justice.

The pressure to be baptized, confirmed and saved was great. Yet the thought of going to a new country, described by my grandmother from the depths of her imagination, sometimes seemed attractive.

My Mother packed on the day of our departure. We were due to catch a boat from Gdynia. My Mother told Pola and gave her money. Distraught, Pola followed us to the railway station, where she clung to me, crying hysterically. She removed the gold cross and chain from round my neck. She called my Mother a thief. Because of me, she had not married or had children of her own. My Mother no longer had exclusive rights over me. Pola had saved my life too many times to let me go and to be brought up a Jew.

They both pulled me towards them on the platform. My Mother took me away and the train left.

part 2

part 2

1

1946—Mary

We arrived in England on August 16th 1946; my Mother, my Grandmother and me. In September my Mother was introduced to a Polish widower, stranded in London since 1939 when he was taking a course in anaesthetics. When war broke out he could not get back home. His whole family had been wiped out. He persuaded me that he had always wanted a little girl like me and so to make his wish come true he was going to marry my Mummy, which he duly did in December. He explained to me that the English were a bit funny about foreigners, so if I was to be happy in England, my English had to be accentless and my manners correct. I had to learn to be a little English girl. He and my Mother went to Thomas Cook & Co's Educational Department and were recommended a small school in Horsham, Sussex where for £28 a term, the process could begin. It was explained to me that under no circumstances was I to reveal that I was Jewish and that I was to work hard at my lessons and do as I was told at all times.

On January 8th 1947, a month short of my eighth birthday, I

found myself on the steps leading to the massive front door of The Causeway School, New Place. The headmistress, Miss Gertrude, led us to the dormitory where I had been assigned a bed. My suitcase was already waiting for me. The precious key was on a cord round my neck. My Mother cried, my new Father hugged me and they left.

I spoke no English. My name was Mary Szczepanska. I had started life as Monika Rosenfeld. When my mother bought forged papers to get us out of the Warsaw ghetto, she changed her name from Edyta Rosenfeld to Krystyna Szczepanska. I was known as Maria or Marysia Szczepanska. When I was taken to Pola in the country, I was passed as her daughter and I became Maria Binkowska. In England, when I was enrolled at The Causeway School, Maria became Mary, but Szczepanska remained—a name that nobody could pronounce. To have one z in a surname would have been considered fanciful, to have two was excessive. My surname was an obstacle course in itself.

Miss Gertrude asked me for the key to my suitcase, showing me what she wanted in smiling mime. After an unseemly struggle she took the key, she opened the case and began to fill my locker with the motley collection of clothes that I had brought. My Mother had assumed that the Uniform List was not compulsory, but meant as kindly suggestions. Its insistence on 'bottle green' translated into Polish, made no sense at all. The job completed, Miss Gertrude led me from the dormitory and terrified, I left my unlocked locker behind me.

For the first time in my life I had nobody to turn to, no Aunt Krysia, now called Mummy when I remembered, and no Pola. I had, however been 'schooled' with tough rules, of which the first was not to share food other than with Pola or Aunt Krysia, and at a pinch, Grandmother. The second most important one was not to let your belongings out of your sight. So when Miss Gertrude asked me for that key, the first Battle of Horsham began.

1946/7 Judith

Leaving St.Helen's school can't have caused me any concern. I know this because I have absolutely no memory of it. David had already left Westcroft to go to City of London school and our mealtimes were dominated by his constant chatter about the teachers and the new boys he had met.

My brother was allowed to travel alone on the tube all the way to the huge, imposing building on the Embankment, where he spent his days learning latin, history and algebra. Once a week all the pupils had to travel to a sports ground, far away in a place called Grove Park. David wasn't much good at games and I usually beat him when we were playing tennis in Gladstone Park with our neighbour, Mr. Cave. I wonder why he was the one to take us there and give us coaching, instead of my mother, who apparently had been a good tennis player. Perhaps you can't play any more when you're old, like forty-four? In one of our games David served quite a fast ball. My swift return to the other side of the court left him standing at the net, gaping at me, swiftly followed by the crack of his racket, as he flung it on the ground.

My new school was called Bute House and it was miles away in Hammersmith. For the first few weeks Mummy took me on the train, changing once from the Bakerloo to the Metropolitan line and then walking up Brook Green to the school. It took about an hour each way. After a few weeks of this, she must have realized that it was taking up nearly four hours of her day, so she found a woman who was happy to be paid to do it. I say 'a woman' because I can't picture her and I never knew her name. All I remember is sitting silently on the tube waiting for the journey to be over.

On the first day we were all lined up for an official photo. The seven or eight year olds, the youngest, were in the front row.

Everyone was wearing the school uniform—white blouses with a Peter Pan collar and pleated navy blue skirts. On the left of the photo, almost in the centre of the front row, was a dark haired girl, trying to smile, but leaning forward to conceal what she was wearing: a patterned cotton dress with short sleeves. This was me, overcome with embarrassment at being the only girl without the uniform. I was told that it had been ordered from Daniel Neal, the supplier, but hadn't arrived in time.

After that school photograph we were allocated classrooms. Of the fifteen teachers I only remember the headmistress, Miss Okeden, and one with blond hair piled on top of her head, Miss Battiscombe. My form mistress remains nameless but I can still hear words pouring out of her mouth, addressing us in a formal tone and often referring to 'our people'. When she asked where my people were from, I didn't understand that she meant the various districts of London. I was struggling to place myself as part of a people and it took me a while to realize that she was talking about my family. What it certainly didn't mean was a group called Jews. I was one of very few Jewish girls at the school and this soon became an enormous problem. Mummy had discussed with the headmistress the fact that I didn't eat meat (she didn't bother to explain the intricacies of kosher meat or the various prohibitions, including shellfish). All that mattered was that I should be allowed to have a vegetarian alternative. This didn't exist. So perhaps I could take sandwiches? No this was not allowed. Everyone had to go into the dining room and eat lunch. Going home to eat was another option, but since the journey took nearly an hour, that was impossible. Mummy came up with a solution.

She found out that in the same road as the school, Brook Green, was a synagogue. Next door lived the Rabbi, a Reverend Venitt.

He agreed to provide a kosher lunch for me every day. All I had to do was walk over there and enjoy what his wife cooked.

Enjoy? This was a disaster. First of all I had to sneak out of school every day while the other girls were lining up to go into lunch. Then I had to sit at a table with two elderly strangers, trying to make conversation and eat unfamiliar food. I was never hungry and although it was probably quite palatable, all I can remember is pushing pieces of meat and overcooked vegetables around my plate, and keeping my eye on the clock to make sure I got back to school in time.

When I went through the gates, my classmates were all standing around in groups, chattering. They were probably continuing the conversations they had started over their pudding and custard. I stood on the side and waited for the bell to ring for the afternoon lessons to begin.

For some reason I endured this for years, never mentioning to my parents that I had a problem. I guess this was because the only solution would have been to change schools, but that didn't seem an option. Bute House was the junior school for the prestigious St. Paul's Girls School, further down the road. The long term plan was for me to go there. Spending a few years at the prep school was the most likely way to succeed.

I couldn't discuss it at school either. How was I to say that 'my people' didn't eat spam fritters or bangers and mash? They wouldn't have understood why I had to go to Mrs. Venitt who was kindly feeding me a different kind of meat and potatoes.

What I Now Know

Many years after I left St. Helen's school I came across some school reports that my mother had kept. To my astonishment I had not spent my days doing very little, but had been studying and tested on fourteen different subjects.

I seemed to have an excellent grasp of dictation, poetry, reading and scripture. My arithmetic was judged 'intelligent' and I seemed to like listening to historical stories. I was even enjoying French and to top it all my writing was very good.

2

Horsham—1947—Mary

The battles ahead were many.

As we left the dormitory, Jane Hodgson came towards us. Round, fair and kind, she had been assigned to look after me and show me the ropes. She smiled and said lots of incomprehensible things and held out her hand, offering me an apple. I knew that if someone offered you food, it could only be for devious motives. I shook my head. She insisted. Miss Gertrude, she who had wrested my key from me, was smiling at us both. I shook my head again. I knew that here was a conspiracy. Jane came closer. I took the apple and threw it very hard at her head.

Remembering that I was not to reveal that I was Jewish, I concentrated on what I did know: that on Sunday everybody in the whole world went to church. I knew so well what to do there that nobody could suspect that I was Jewish, though I was not sure what 'Jewish' was about. Pola had threatened eternal damnation if I stayed that way. My new Father had told me that it was a good thing, but that it could be dangerous to tell anybody about it. I was confused.

That first Sunday morning we formed a neat crocodile and went off to church, a dour Victorian gothic building with no statues, no decoration, no candles and no colour. There was no font for Holy Water so I began to cross myself vigorously without it. Pola would have been proud. An arm came out trying to stop me. There was no procession and no nice smell. It was all very odd but I launched into Ave Maria, gratia plena, Dominus tecum… in mulieribus… loud enough to be heard, as I had been taught to do. I was word perfect.

Many years later my Father told me that he had been telephoned by an indignant Miss Gertrude who asked why she had not been informed that I was Catholic and that I had embarrassed the whole school. He, in his turn, had been embarrassed that he had completely forgotten about the Protestant/Catholic divide in the United Kingdom. There were so many more important matters he had to consider in his life.

For me too, there were more new things to deal with. Little girls undressed and washed in freezing bathrooms. In the cold of Polish winters I had learnt to uncover a little bit at a time, wash it and cover it up quickly before moving on to the next bit. That was unacceptable. Little girls were sent out to play in the snow with one pair of socks and wellington boots and spent the nights crying with pain, rubbing their inflamed chilblains. I knew I had to wear two pairs of socks with carefully arranged layers of newspaper between the two before I put on my boots. That was unladylike and unacceptable. Little girls had to share, though I quickly noticed that all the little girls' butter ration was in dishes on the staff table whilst the margarine ration was generously left for us.

My parents had saved their sweet ration and one or two friends had also contributed coupons as a going-to-school present. They had sent me off with four bars of chocolate in my toy box but these were quickly spotted and confiscated. I was invited to share the chocolate with my new classmates. The teacher broke it into pieces and handed the squares round the room, popping more than one into her own mouth. She then asked the girls to come up in turn, introduce themselves and take two squares each. As the first girl, Nichola, stepped forward. she stretched her hand towards the chocolate and said "Thank you very much Mary. My name is Nichola." The full enormity of what was happening came upon me like a scalding shower. They were going to take my chocolate, my food. This was something for which one fought to the death because without it, death was inevitable anyway. They had taken my clothes and now they were going to take my food.

My despair was total and nobody comforted my tears because I should have been smiling at the pleasure my chocolate was giving. My obvious lack of generosity was not acceptable.

The school was focused on horses and gymkhanas. One or two of the girls came with their own ponies which they were allowed to ride every day. Rosettes were proudly displayed in the dining room and along the corridors. I, meanwhile, had very quickly learned that a nod and a smile were always very well received so even if I did not understand a word, I nodded and smiled most of the time. In a school so focused on horses, it was not altogether surprising that something of the reputation of the brave and colourful Polish Cavalry had seeped into Horsham. Being Polish, it was assumed that I was the daughter of the cavalry and had probably mounted a horse before I could walk. Somebody must have asked me a question and I must have smiled and nodded because soon after arriving at the school I was led to the stables in triumph and invited to get up on a huge beast. I was given a leg up, my reluctance ignored. The horse moved. I fell off.

Without language, without help or explanation, it was difficult to work out what I was not allowed to do or why I was not allowed to do it. I had no concept of arbitrary School Rules. Rules to me had always been connected to survival.

Here they seemed to have a different meaning.

There were two staircases in the building. The staff and the prefects were allowed to use the magnificent, polished oak stairs with the carved newel posts at the top and the bottom. The rest of us had to use the servants' staircase, so-called from the days when the building had been a manor house. Steep and narrow, it was often jammed when one class was going up and another was trying to go down. The oak staircase meanwhile remained broad, haughty and empty. Since there was no 'man-with-a-machine-gun' at either end, just newel posts at the top and the bottom, I used that.

What I Now Know

Survival: The only thing that mattered in my world was to be geared up for survival. In order to have a better chance, I had to be able to blend in as English. I was playing a role in a play I had not written, one that had every chance of coming to a sticky end as it had for all our families.

Thinking about those first months at The Causeway school I realize it was not just the lack of English that made communication hard. There was so much that I couldn't talk about: the running and the hiding, my friend shot in the stomach while I was walking with him, trying to stuff his guts back into the gaping hole with my hands, the smell of burning flesh and of fear, the screaming and the hunger, the cellars and the bombing and the stench of people too close together for too long. All these were forbidden subjects. First of all I did not know the words to describe them, then I did not know if I could talk about it at all. Then later, when I began to try to comprehend the feelings of people around me, they just seemed trivial and childish. I realized that we were divided by more than language. And I did not mind. Really, I did not want to talk about any of it, neither to them, nor to my parents.

After the first term I was allowed to travel to school on my own so the journeys with 'the woman' came to an end. I sat on the train with the pupils from Godolphin and Latymer and the Sacred Heart Catholic School. I was transfixed by some of the girls who had long hair, often piled in a bun on top of their head. I worked out that they must have been in a ballet school because of the way they walked and held themselves. They simply looked soignée, a word I probably learned much later.

Like many of the girls at Bute House, I had short hair. A few had 'bunches' or plaits, but the prevailing style was short, with a side parting. My mother, concerned for her daughter's appearance, convinced herself that I needed to have curly hair. To that end she made me stand, every evening before I went to bed, while she wrapped sections of my hair in rags, cut from an old sheet. She twisted the cotton and made a knot to keep each one in place. In the morning when the rags were taken out, I woke up with wavy hair. I must have complained about this on two counts: first because it was tedious standing there while it was being done, and then because the cotton knots all over my head made it hard to get comfortable on the pillow to go to sleep.

Protesting that I wanted plaits was no solution. Mummy didn't want me to have long hair. But I solved this. Finally refusing to have my hair in rags, I went to her knitting bag and found balls of brown wool. I took them back to my bedroom and cut the wool into foot long pieces. Then I plaited them neatly into two thick braids. Every evening after supper I would disappear to my room and fix the home made plaits to my hair, swinging them from side to side, feeling the swish of the false hair on my face. When I got tired I always remembered to push the 'plaits' down under the bedclothes so no-one would find them.

Having wavy hair made no difference to whether or not I made friends. Everyone needed to have a 'best friend' but this proved hard for a child who was shy, possibly fearing rejection. Even the question of my name seemed a problem. We were often asked to write or call out our 'Christian name' and to me the names I heard, Penelope or Arabella, sounded posh. At primary school my friends were called Ruth and Sarah, while some parents—perhaps wanting to be more modern—had discarded Biblical names and called their daughters Sandra or Brenda.

The girls at Bute House lived in homes in Richmond or Roehampton, places I had never been to. I'd just about heard of Chiswick because it was on one of the train lines, but everything South of the river was unfamiliar. Somehow I knew that these were not areas like Kilburn and Willesden Green. I conjured up an image of mansions set in parkland, while I overheard conversations at break time. Serena and Heather used to talk about an exclusive tennis club called the Hurlingham and I wondered what they would have thought of the few hard courts at Gladstone Park, where I had my first lessons.

There was constant chatter about dresses. Most of the mothers bought their daughters frocks at C & A, so occasionally two girls would turn up at a party wearing the same thing. My clothes were exclusively home-made—in my mind, quite inferior to the bought ones. I begged Mummy to let me get one from C & A but she dismissed my request with the words 'Cheap and Awful, that's what it stands for.'

I found myself hanging around on the fringes of a group who all seemed to be enthralled by a girl called Rhona. She was pretty with long eyelashes. She had a particularly nice skin colour. It wasn't exactly a tan, but it wasn't like my pale complexion. There was another thing that made us all want to be in her group. She had secrets. Occasionally she would tell a secret to one of us, separately, in return for a favour of some kind: going to fetch things for her, or telling her the answers in an arithmetic test.

The secrets were never fully revealed. There were hints, winks and the promise of a revelation. I don't know where Rhona found them, but she had a stash of a magazine called Health and Efficiency. It was supposed to be about topics such as exercise and diet, but there were some pictures of naked people. If you were in Rhona's clique she would show you one of these and hint that it was linked to the 'big secret' or 'facts of life' as they were known.

I can safely say that in all my years cultivating Rhona and her courtiers, I never discovered the secret of reproduction or anything else that grown-ups seemed to know about.

3

Although neither my Mother nor my Father had told me to do so, I took it as a given that I had to have a hiding place. Within the first few days at the school I knew I would not find one in the house. This was the first time that I would have to fend for myself. Until now either Pola or Auntie Krysia had found one for me. When I had moved into my new father's little flat with my mother I had seen at a glance that the top of one of the fitted wardrobes was exactly my size and that I could be thrown up there in the twinkling of an eye should there be a knock at the door. Before that, hiding was taken as much for granted as breathing. Whenever we had moved, from Łódz to Warsaw, from Warsaw to the countryside and then back again, whether with Auntie Krysia or with Pola, the first thing they had always done was to find a hiding place for me. Once it had been in a deep drawer. Another time they had half emptied a mattress and left one end open for me. Here, in the school I had found nothing so I decided to look in the grounds.

I had to protect myself from the soldiers. The fact that I had not seen any soldiers since our arrival in England was no proof that they were not lurking somewhere. I had looked for a hiding place in the stables but I was frightened of getting too close to the horses and the tack room was locked at night, so I had given that up as an idea. There were big broom cupboards and storage areas around the kitchen but if there was to be a raid, I decided that it would be better to be out of the main building. There were lots of places in the grounds, up trees and in the bushes, but I wanted somewhere that could be useful in the winter, as well as in the summer. Finally, I spotted the sacks in the greenhouse.

One of the many rules that I could not understand was that there was to be no talking once the lights were turned off in the dormitories. 'Silence!' is an order difficult for a group of small girls to obey, especially in the summer when we were put to bed too early, with the sun still shining outside. By the time the first summer in Horsham came, I understood enough English to know what that barked order meant.

'Good night and sleep tight. And SILENCE!!'

I did not know enough English to ask why. Still, when the other girls whispered and giggled, I giggled. Miss Gertrude went on a late round and caught us. She came in looking grim, told us to get out of bed, put on our dressing gowns, strip our beds and follow her. As usual, I copied what the other girls did. She led us down the corridors and opened the door to a classroom where one girl was invited to step in. The light was then turned off and the door closed. One by one we were isolated in dark, empty classrooms.

It did not occur to me that this was the punishment for giggling and whispering. No grown up person I knew would do that. I had never been punished for disobedience because I had never disobeyed. I knew from experience, however, that silence was vital when the enemy was at the door. I had not seen the men in either black or green uniforms but I assumed that Miss Gertrude had. I could not understand why she thought that a dark classroom made it a place of safety.

Why had she separated us out in our dressing gowns? I knew that I had to disappear so I slipped out of the classroom out of the building and made my way to the greenhouse. I snuggled into the sacks, covered myself and eventually fell asleep.

When eventually I crept out, late in the morning, I knew that I had evaded capture. The enemy must have been and gone without me. Pola would be so proud of me when I told her about it but I never did see her again to tell her of my genius.

What I Now Know

Separation: For me, to be separated or picked out was a kind of selection. In my mind, this was always terrifying, reminding me of events I had witnessed or experienced.

Many years later Miss Gertrude told me of the panic I had caused when she discovered I was missing. She had merely intended to open the door to let me out of the classroom and send me, duly punished, back to bed, as she had the other girls.

1948—Judith

Twice a week, when the school day ended, I didn't go straight home. From the station I went to the synagogue at the corner of Walm Lane for Hebrew classes. These also happened on Sunday mornings but it's the weekday ones that stuck in my mind, with a memory of a horrid bun that almost stuck in my throat.

Because we didn't have time to go home, we were given something to eat at the classes before the lesson began. It was always the same: a sticky poppy seed roll with a taste of mixed spice. As I was so hungry I stuffed the stale bun into my mouth and then had to spend the next ten minutes trying to pick the black seeds out of my teeth.

It was at the classes that I met the boys. Derek and his brother lived in the next street. They went to the local school and had scuffed shoes and black hair that was smoothed down with Brilliantine. I chose to sit next to them while we were writing Hebrew letters on a page. If we got them wrong the teacher would hit us with his rolled up newspaper. At the end of each class we did some singing and dancing. I think the songs were about the brave pioneers in the deserts of Israel. I got to know the words and the steps as we formed circles in the hall. Finally it was time to go home. My house was just a five minute walk away but I would often stroll on a bit further with the boys and then wave goodbye before turning back again. I could hear them giggling and saying words I'd never heard before.

At school I was enjoying the early signs of summer. We played rounders on the grass and because I was good at running I was often one of the first to be picked for a team. (The biggest humiliation of course, was to be left standing on the side when most of the players had been chosen).

Games have rules and we quickly picked them up. Basically, one team bats while the other team fields and bowls. If you are batting you have to run to as many posts as possible, before the fielders can get the ball to touch the post first. I won't go into the details of how you score a Rounder or a half Rounder.

There were long stretches of time sitting out and waiting for our turn but when I got to the crease and batted the ball high in the air, it was so good to feel the wind in my hair as I ran past first and second post. The girls called out 'Well played' and for the first time I didn't feel 'out of it.'

It was coming up to my 9th birthday. Mummy promised me a party. I knew she would make wonderful food: little sandwiches with the crusts cut off, chocolate eclairs, meringues and cake. She had learned to make all these things at the Cordon Bleu after she left university and was, as she told me laughingly, a 'skilled pâtissière'.

We wrote out the invitations and sent them to a dozen girls in my class. The replies came back, one after the other, saying that Cricklewood was too far away, or they were busy. Only two girls accepted. To make up for the lack of school friends I decided to invite Derek and his brother and told them about the birthday party next time I saw them at Hebrew classes. Then I told my mother. I wasn't quite expecting such a horror-stricken reaction. She'd heard me talking about the boys and had formed a picture of them in her mind that made them totally unsuitable company for the couple of girls from Bute House. She tried to explain that it was possible to move in two worlds, but trying to create a social mix of people from contrasting backgrounds needed more skill than her daughter had at that age.

The party was a disaster. I told the boys they weren't invited after all and was left with the two girls who had accepted. We played games and then sat down to tea, starting with sandwiches, cut into fancy shapes. The guests wanted to know what the fillings were. They were hoping for Marmite or jam. What they were offered was cod's roe, cream cheese with olive, or egg and anchovy. Their plates remained untouched. Mummy cleared the table and brought out the cake. She had been saving the sugar ration for two weeks and had produced a sponge filled with strawberries and a custardy cream. I was wishing she had bought a Dundee cake and a plate of Penguin biscuits.

What I Now Know

My mother was, indeed, an excellent cook, but she only ever taught me how to make one thing, soon after I was married. She stood in my kitchen and showed me the intricacies of puff pastry.

4

Horsham—Mary

It was as I began to understand English that I came to the conclusion that the children around me were unbelievably childish. They talked about brothers and sisters and new bicycles and ponies and the seaside and parties and puppies. I rapidly understood that any mention of guns and rats and bodies and black uniforms would be considered nasty and fanciful. I had nothing to contribute to their chatter.

I learnt to read and found what was appropriate in the school tales of Enid Blyton. All the stalwart heroines were called Susan and Jennifer and the mean, bossy prefect was Monica, a name that was mine somewhere but which I was not allowed to use. Reading Enid Blyton, I could see why.

Telling the truth when questioned by the authorities, if the truth pointed to the sins of another girl, was considered telling tales and was thus unacceptable. Owning up bravely to your own misdeeds was the right thing to do and more than acceptable. It was honourable: new word.

It was bad form to be clever, a swot, but could be redeemed by being good at team sports, hockey or netball. Tennis was hardly mentioned because that demanded individual prowess and could lead to showing off and making an exhibition of yourself, which was very bad form.

In daily life I learnt that sharing your pencils was good form and that helping people who had not done their homework was the team spirit expected by your classmates. But offering sweets from your weekly sweet ration, especially to an older girl, was very bad form because that could be construed as sucking up which was even worse than showing off.

Whether from Enid Blyton or by always looking around me, I learnt that there were things that you said and things that you did that were beyond question because nobody nice had ever questioned them. So I learnt to queue and to wait for my turn. I learnt not to make a fuss. I learnt that when my parents came on Visiting Sunday it was terribly bad form to run sobbing into their arms; so foreign and dramatic.

Both Aunt Pola and Aunt Krysia had encouraged me to be brave. They had often told me that I was brave. They had praised me. I learnt that that word of praise in Polish did not translate into the English of Horsham, Sussex. I tried to learn every rule of the complicated gavotte of daily life because both my Mother and my new Father had given me to understand that this was survival, new rules to take the place of the rules I had learnt in Poland, which were now out of date. This is what I had to absorb in order to survive in England.

1948—Judith

The form mistress handed me a note to take home to my parents. They were summoned to a meeting at the school to discuss an 'important matter'. I wasn't in the headmistress's study when she had a conversation with my mother about my progress. The issue that had prompted the note was my sewing. Apparently I couldn't do cross stitch. Mummy smiled with relief and asked why she had been brought all the way from Cricklewood to be told that. Regretting her sharp reaction, she changed her tone: "I'm sorry she can't do cross stitch. Is there a problem with her maths and spelling too?"

The following term Mummy was summoned to the school again. This time it was more serious. I had been doing something very, very bad. I suppose it was called stealing, but I thought of it as borrowing. It started when I was in the cloakroom after the others had all gone home. We each had a peg and a locker. On the peg was a shoebag where we kept our indoor shoes and plimsolls. One day I looked on the floor and saw a pair of shiny patent shoes. I had a vague memory of owning shoes like that when I was a small girl, but during the war I never saw anything fancy. I picked up one of the black shoes and slipped the strap over the button, then my eyes went to my own brown sandals. I don't know what made me do it, but I scooped up the black pumps, pushed them into my shoebag and hung it back on the peg.

Days passed and everyone in the class was asked to search for the lost shoes. I kept quiet. I added more items to the bag with the name Judith. There was a leather purse with punched holes and a small box of Caran d'Ache crayons. These bright coloured pencils were the most desirable things to own. They weren't available in England and the only way you could get them was if you knew someone who was going to Switzerland. Now I had them.

I must have taken the shoebag home but I never took out my treasures. Every day the bag with its contents was returned to the peg. My stupidity was soon discovered. Mummy was again called in to speak to the Headmistress, who was sitting behind her desk, eyeing my shoebag. She handed it to me and asked me to tip out the contents. This time my mother had no witty response. She was ashamed and upset. I was silent.

We spoke little on the way home because I had nothing to say: I'd made the apologies to the Headmistress but I had no explanation and no excuse. When I got to the house I rushed into the kitchen to tell Beatis what had happened.

She was in the middle of ironing. I flung myself, sobbing, into her arms. She patted my back and whispered soothing words. She never asked the question "Why?"

Beatis had been a maid 'in service' since she was fifteen. She came to work for my grandmother, and then my mother, but no longer lived in, coming just a couple of times a week to help with light tasks like ironing and washing up. I never remember my mother having a 'cleaner'—she and Beatis shared the tasks like washing floors and changing beds. Beatis enjoyed cleaning silver, so that was another time when I would sit talking to her as she polished cutlery and candlesticks till they shone.

One day she seemed a bit quiet. I didn't think to ask her if anything was wrong, but she told me anyway. Her only son Bernard—the one in the RAF—was about to emigrate to Australia. That was the only time I saw her cry. She said very little. I didn't understand what she was saying about 'having no choice' and 'accepting his decision.' I did take in her last words on the subject: "We'll probably never see him again." It was Daddy who explained to me the finality of Bernard's decision to leave England.

It was strange because I rarely had important conversations with my father. I think my parents were simply too pre-occupied, first with the war and then with the rationing and austerity that continued for years afterwards.

I have to explain here that my father was much older than my mother—and almost any other father I knew. He didn't get married till he was in his fifties. When David and I were born he was clearly overjoyed. He never actually told me but I could see it from photos on the sideboard, where he was beaming at a baby in a pram or holding the reins when we were toddlers. At night he would sit by my bed and say my prayers with me:

Blessed be the Lord by day, blessed be the Lord by night.

Blessed be the Lord when we lie down......

Shema Yisrael, Hear O Israel, the Lord is our God the Lord is one.

Although he walked a lot he wasn't what you would call active and had little interest in my sporting activities. David's academic progress and his interest in debating were probably more up his street. Unlike most husbands, he left planning, holidays and driving to my mother. He was happy to be left to read and if it had been up to him they would never have gone out.

What I Now Know

I didn't realize till I married how much I loved Beatis. I used to visit her in her small council house in Burnt Oak, near the more prosperous suburb of Edgware. By this time she was widowed, living alone in a meticulously kept living room and bedroom. She had few possessions, the small ornaments on the sideboard dominated by the large photo of Bernard in his RAF uniform. She was right in her fear that she would never see him again. In those days it was impossible for the average person to find the money for the fare to Australia.

Just before my wedding Beatis talked about buying us a present. I didn't want her to, knowing she had little money, but she insisted. The conversation was difficult and as I sat in one of her two armchairs I noticed an old copper kettle on a shelf in the room. "That's what I would like" I said. Beatis laughed, saying it was an old thing, not nearly as good as the new electric ones. I have it still, on a shelf with all my cookbooks, and when I polish the copper I think of the hours we spent together.

5

After a while I stopped crying for Pola. My Mother answered reluctantly when I asked when she was coming to live with us in London. In the end she told me that Pola had decided to stay in Poland. I believed her.

My Father paid for piano lessons because he considered that to be an acceptable accomplishment. I played badly and was not allowed to give up for many years. He did not agree to ballet lessons because he considered it would be unlikely that I would ever be asked to entertain at a dinner party with my rendering of The Dying Swan. I went to Greek Dancing lessons on Saturday because for those there was no extra charge. They were good for deportment. Although I did not ride after the first miserable experiment, I learnt to talk about gymkhanas, help clean the stables and admire the rosettes. I learnt to make daisy chains and to enquire after brothers, sisters, cousins and, of course, the puppies.

Lessons were an obstacle course at first. At the beginning a bright teacher gave me a mark for every word I got right, where the rest of the class lost a mark for every spelling mistake. One of the problems that a small, underfunded boarding school had, and there must have been a great many problems, was the turnover of teachers. For one term and one term only, there was an elderly lady called Miss Barton. She taught English and she was the first to open my mind to the beauty of this language that was to nourish me for the rest of my life. I wrote a composition and used the only adjective I knew, 'nice'. I attached it to every noun I knew and there were not a lot of those, so she sat me next to her and together we looked at a table and I learnt that it was small, square, green, shiny, heavy. It was a great many things except, perhaps, nice. She told me that English had so many words and I could play with them all, mix and match and even make them rhyme.

Every six weeks we were allowed to go home for a long week-end. Then there were the Christmas holidays, the Easter holidays and the long summer holidays, all spent in London, all lived in Polish.

At school we ate more for training in table manners than for nourishment. The food was awful and there was not a lot of it except for mountains of sliced white bread called Wonderloaf. We were not allowed to reach out and take a slice but had to wait for a considerate neighbour to notice that our plate was empty and to offer the basket with the magic sentence 'Would you like some bread?' whereupon we could take one slice and one slice only. There was much kicking under the table and much room for revenge built into the system.

At home we ate our evening meals at a small table in the hall that served as dining room, sitting room and office. My Mother passed the large bowls of soup. I looked longingly at the bread. My parents, deep in conversation, did not notice my attention seeking little coughs. They were ignoring my need in the rudest possible manner according to Horsham Rules.

"Would you like some bread" I asked my Father hoping for some reciprocity.

"No." he said, a little puzzled, and carried on the conversation with my Mother.

I offered my Mother some bread but she was so engrossed that she did not bother to reply. Finally, out of desperation, I did the unforgiveable. I asked my Father if he would pass the bread. He looked at me and at the plate of bread, some nine inches from my hand. "Tell me," he said, "have you arms shrunk this term at school?"

Being an English miss did not fit home rules.

1949—Judith

When it was time for the last of the school photos—there must have been one every year—things had improved at Bute House. The ethos of the school was that we should all be kind to each other, so attempts were made by the staff not to allow cliques or bullying. Of course, no-one was seriously excluded or made to feel unhappy and my personal list of embarrassments started to recede into the background. Whatever deep distress had caused my episodes of stealing had been forgotten.

The biggest change as I passed three birthdays was that we began to have a sense of humour about the school rules and activities that were compulsory. Included in the timetable was a fitness regime called Eurythmics. The teachers took it seriously, but for us the weird movements were comical and ridiculous.

Perhaps, because I have little memory of the actual school day and the work we did in class, it signifies that I was easily keeping up with the others, maybe even excelling in subjects like spelling and arithmetic. And, perhaps I wasn't so funny looking either. And I had a secret. I had a new friend at home.

At about this time an Italian family came into our lives. I say 'came in' because they simply turned up at our home and were there several days a week. Apparently the father had been a friend of my mother's, in the 1930s. The story, as I knew it, was that during the war the Benzimras had been hiding in France and were now coming to live in England. They were looking for a school for their only son, Lyon. Since he was the same age as my brother David, it was decided that he should go to City of London.

At home there was much talk of 'entrance exams' and 'quotas'. It was difficult to get into St. Paul's and for certain other schools there was a quota of the number of pupils who were of a different faith from the prevailing C of E. I have no idea how Lyon got into City of London but I assume that because of the problems they had come from, the procedure was slightly different.

I was fascinated by this family. Walter Benzimra was tall and good looking. Before they escaped to France he had qualified as a doctor in Italy but was also an artist of considerable talent. Their home was in Palace Gardens Terrace in Kensington—a slightly ramshackle house on many floors. There was antique furniture and paintings on every inch of space on the walls. For me there was something exciting: a small lift that went from the kitchen down to the dining room where Violette served the best pasta I have ever eaten.

Lyon had straight brown hair, glasses and a serious expression. He was also fun because he had a great skill—drawing. He was able to sketch portraits in minutes and also to play a game where someone drew a squiggle on a piece of paper and he would turn it into an animal.

While we played I was aware that there were some serious discussions going on. There were hints at what had happened to them but the details were never discussed. We just talked about school.

I had no door key, so I always rang the bell at home. One day there was no answer. It took a few minutes before my father opened the door. He told me Mummy was not feeling well. Over the next few days she became seriously ill, unable to stand or walk as she was suffering from extreme giddiness. It turned out that this was Ménière's Disease, apparently a 'disorder of the inner ear'. Mummy could hardly talk; all she would say was "the world is spinning round". Days and weeks passed. She couldn't even lift her head from the pillow. She had lost her balance and hours of extreme nausea were followed by anxiety and fatigue. At night I lay in bed in a panic. I was convinced she was going to die. I don't know how many weeks it took for the disease to subside. There is no cure but eventually it does go away. My fear of being left without her took many years to pass.

When she was well we went on a holiday. Daddy took his bellows camera. I think it was brown leather with a strap that was constantly round his neck. I spoiled his pleasure in taking photos because like many young girls I would turn away to avoid being in the picture. Mummy avoided having her ample figure recorded by hiding behind someone else who was pushed to the foreground.

Pesach was coming. We used the Hebrew word and never called it by the English name Passover. It's too complicated to explain the reason here but we needed to change all our plates for the week of the Festival. Daddy came home with a large box full of brand new white plates. The only problem was that each one had a prominent emblem on the side 'P & P.' We were assured that this referred to the words Pesach and Passover. David muttered that they must have belonged to a company that had gone out of business. At mealtimes we joked about the possible names of the directors—all beginning with a P.

At Bute House we were beginning to look forward to our lives at 'the big school'. Some of the girls had older sisters who were attending St. Paul's, so we knew that rounders would be replaced by cricket, netball and lacrosse. In our work timetable we would soon be on a path to making choices for ourselves, a dramatic change once we entered the Senior School.

There must have been an entrance exam for the Senior School, but strangely I have no recollection of it. It was only a year or two later that I have any memory of sitting in a room with dozens of desks and a teacher walking round putting exam papers in front of us. Perhaps the transition was done by interview. Is it possible that I went to meet the staff at the Senior School to answer questions that would determine my suitability for the superior education they were offering? I do have a memory of sheer astonishment when, a few terms later, I walked through the dark wood doors leading to the main hall at St. Paul's. Hundreds of chairs were arranged in rows. At the far end was a platform and behind that the organ. On either side of the hall were the classrooms and above it all was the balcony with more rooms, perhaps including the High Mistress's study. Maybe it was here that my work had been evaluated and I was deemed fit to become a 'Paulina'?

The summer term came and went. I stood in the back row, with friends, waiting for the click of the photographer's shutter. Something about that photo revealed that I had a new found confidence, having obtained a place at St. Paul's. My parents were overjoyed. David was a bit put out because he was no longer the only one who could talk about debating societies and prize days. The next stage of my life was about to begin.

On a bright September day, equipped with the right uniform this time, I arrived at the gates of the Senior School and walked inside, threading my way through a crowd of new girls, hoping to find someone to walk with. It surely wouldn't be good to step through those vast wooden doors alone. I walked up a few steps so I could get a better view of the newcomers. There was a girl with thick dark plaits carrying a very unusual satchel. It was brand new, made of tan-coloured pigskin and was by far the best looking satchel I had ever seen. She had short legs, bright white socks and shiny shoes. When I looked at her face, she looked back at me and gave me a smile. "Shall we go in together?" she asked. "Why not?" I replied.

6

My Father told me that I was to take an entrance exam to a very good school in London. I would be leaving Horsham and coming to live at home. One of his patients had told him that he should try to get me into St. Paul's School for Girls. Fortunately he did not know what a challenge that would be, that places were sought after and that there would be competition. It was not till many years later that he found out that the same patient, in possession of a title and a famous family name, had written to the High Mistress explaining the circumstances and asking her to look beyond the entrance exam where I could not help but do badly.

Miss Gertrude was asked to prepare me for the exam but no little girl from her school had done such a thing. Academic excellence was not an important item on the list of the school's virtues. I had learned how to do chain stitch and satin stitch, how to darn my socks neatly and how to cut out and sew a pair of baggy knickers using a French hem. But she had no idea what would be demanded of me at this London school that demanded fancy entrance exams. She made no effort to find out; for instance, she was informed that I had to have some knowledge of geography so she gave me a map of England, shut me in a room and told me to learn it. Where to begin? I knew that when I wrote a composition I had to go easy on the word nice and when I drew a line, I had to use a ruler.

When the day came, I had no idea how important this exam was; I am not quite sure if I knew what the word 'exam' meant. At the end of the day, after I had written a Composition and done a few sums I was summoned to see the High Mistress in her office. She asked me if I missed Poland. She asked me if I liked my school in Horsham and if I was getting on well there. My answers were constrained by the rules of no boasting and not making an exhibition of yourself so I felt I could not tell her about the good marks I was getting for Composition and that I had scored a goal in the last netball game. She asked me why I wanted to come to St. Paul's and with the seriousness of a judge I explained to her that my Father had told me that I had to have a very good education because I had no family to rely on and would always have to earn my own living when I grew up. It would be her job to provide that education. It had never occurred to me that the exam I had sat or the meeting with this interesting woman had any bearing on my being admitted to the school. Miss Osborne smiled and told me that she was sure I would be very happy at St. Paul's and that I could start in September.

This time my Mother understood that the Uniform List had to be complete. I had every single item. On September 11th I woke up before dawn, dressed carefully; shiny shoes, blue tunic, navy blue coat all topped off with a black hat with the proud school badge embroidered on the front. I waited in a chair clutching my beautiful brief case. I must have dozed off.

It was on the steps leading to the imposing front door of the school, surrounded by the other new girls, also in their pristine navy coats and hats, that I saw Judy for the first time.

the meeting

Judith

I was the child of an educated Jewish family, sure of its identity and its roots. My parents had both been in England for decades. My mother, of Portuguese descent, was a maths graduate and a teacher; my father was a chemical engineer and a patent agent. My older brother David was clever and argumentative. He made us laugh. The path set out for us both was to go to good schools where we would have a sense of belonging and come out with an education that would ensure a bright future.

For us the war had been something to be endured with patience and calm. Though everyone lived in fear of a German invasion, it was food rationing, the blackout and the Blitz that dominated our lives. Living in Britain meant following the rules without complaint. Enemy bombing claimed many lives in the cities and some families decided to leave the vulnerable towns and seek refuge in less targeted areas. School age children were being evacuated on their own to live in new and strange families, but for us this was not an option: we were too young for it to be considered.

My life was punctuated by attending synagogue and saying evening prayers with my father. Our family celebrated New Year, Passover and the other Festivals. I simply knew that I was English and Jewish.

My days at the local primary school were uneventful so it came as a shock when I transferred to a junior school far away, with unfamiliar girls and little tolerance of Jewish practices. Three years later I was ready for a new experience, but standing alone while other girls chattered like excited starlings, I was none the less apprehensive.

Monika

Few people had the prescience to leave to seek refuge elsewhere. My parents had stayed. My father had been shot in the Radogoszcz Woods.

I had grown up with fear, persecuted for reasons I did not begin to understand. I accepted the fear as the normal order of things. I had known nothing of my parentage other than that I had two 'Aunties' who looked after me in turn. Even my first name had been changed, from Monika to Mary. I was affectionately called Marysia. I knew nothing of religion and the concept of 'Jews' or being 'Jewish' had not yet crossed my childhood consciousness. Meanwhile from one of the Aunties I learned to cross myself in church and I knew that when the war was over I would be saved from eternal hell by being baptised.

In London I had waited fruitlessly with my mother and grandmother for a ship that would take us on to Chile. Just before my eighth birthday, with my mother newly married, I was packed off to a country boarding school in Sussex. It was only then that I was told I was Jewish. It was a dark secret never to be revealed to anyone else. No-one could be sure that the Gestapo had disappeared for ever.

Speaking only Polish and with no Auntie to help, I had been faced with incomprehensible regulations. Unlike the English girls who had been brought up to obey rules set down by teachers, my encounters with authority had always been accompanied by the threat of weapons.

Three years at the boarding school had taught me a new code of acceptable behaviour. I emerged as a fair imitation of a nice middle class British child. I spoke English with no trace of a foreign accent. Mealtimes had offered dire food and little enjoyment, but I had at least learned good table manners. My handling of a knife and fork was faultless.

Judith

Monika and I first met on the steps of our new school in 1950. We were eleven years old, coming from different backgrounds but with one thing in common. We were both about to change our names and emerge into a different personality.

Most first meetings are significant. This one was not. The encounter seemed almost matter-of-fact. My mind hadn't yet turned to finding friends at the new school. I looked around me and saw groups of girls, hoping to choose one I could walk with through the imposing oak door. I saw Monika: a happy, confident girl carrying an enviable pigskin satchel. She had thick dark plaits, a hairstyle I had always wanted but never achieved. We walked through together.

Monika

There we were on the steps of St. Paul's Girls' School, a gaggle of small girls waiting to be ushered into the temple of learning; the fortunate bright ones who had won the right to be there. I do not remember how I had managed to persuade my Mother not to wait with me but to my great relief, she was not standing next to me. It would have been impossible to pass as a bona fide English schoolgirl with her at my side, wearing clothes that no sensible English mother would have worn before the cocktail hour; very high heels and a bit of feathery, flowery nonsense on her head.

The girls all wore hats with the magic letters SPS embroidered in white on a black ribbon. I had slept with mine on the pillow next to me. We each had a new coat, white socks, black shining shoes and a smart container for books, a satchel or a brief case. Mine was a very expensive gift from my Aunt in America.

The girls who had been to the junior school were less nervous than those of us who had come from other schools. They knew each other and some of them were talking as if to be on those stone steps was the most natural thing in the world. Judy had been to the junior school but she seemed to be as anxious as I felt. I noticed her but did not dare talk to her. We walked in together.

Judith

Monika and I spoke tentatively to each other. When the heavy oak doors opened, it seemed natural to walk through them together. We found ourselves in one of three parallel classes for the incoming girls. We became friends. I admired Monika's quick response to a 'put down' where I slunk away in silence. She wore beautiful dresses, mine were made at home by my mother.

I don't remember how or when we started talking about the past.

I didn't know then - and only discovered when we were seventeen - that this girl had endured a horrific childhood in Poland during the war. She may have said something about the subsequent time when, as an eight year old, she was sent to an English boarding school. She might have mentioned that she had no knowledge of the language but would not have revealed the aspects of her prior life that made it impossible to fit in with either the pupils or the staff.

Monika

Judy seemed so serene. She had neatly cut sandwiches for her mid-morning break - I had biscuit money. She had pretty sprigged cotton dresses made by her mother. I had transparent organza dresses with broderie anglaise sent by my aunt from Saks Fifth Avenue; party dresses that made me feel ridiculous. She was slim and sporty and never had comments 'Careless' and 'Could do better' scrawled across the bottom of her homework.

Judy

For the next six years our lives were filled with conversation. Whether lazing in the cricket nets making daisy chains, or muttering complaints about the vegetarian lunch of inedible jacket potatoes filled with tinned spaghetti, our mouths were hardly ever still. We were either chatting, eating or even singing, be it hymns at morning assembly or in ambitious choirs in the massive singing hall where eminent conductors were brought in to guide our efforts.

After school we went to each other's homes. My mother, who was a large woman wearing little make up, would welcome us with dainty sandwiches with the crusts removed and a home made cake. I rarely saw Monika's mother. She would sometimes appear, coming out of the bedroom; blonde and sad and glamorous, speaking English with a heavy accent.

Monika

I dreaded Judy coming to my home. As often as not my Mother was resting in the bedroom and would emerge reluctantly in her dressing gown. She was always tired. Judy's home was so comfortable. We had a 'salon' with beautiful antique furniture which was for visitors, and covered with plastic when there were no visitors, which was most of the time. Life was lived round the red formica kitchen table. Judy never made any comment about the bread, butter and jam I put on the table, and the shop-bought cake.

She never asked me awkward questions, something I always dreaded when I visited my new friends from the school. I had been invited to the home of another new friend whose grandparents had left Poland in the 1930s. They asked me why my parents had not had the foresight to leave. I did not know. They asked me if they had stayed because they were attached to their good furniture and Persian rugs. I did not know. But I did know that these parents thought of mine as exceptionally stupid and short sighted. I was unsettled and uncomfortable but I knew not to ask my parents for what stupid reason they had not left Poland in time.

Judy

My mother was older than Monika's mother and my father was old enough to be my grandfather. But we did not go to each other's homes to see the parents. We were there because we wanted to carry on talking or to go to see a film together or to discuss which subjects we wanted to choose for our GCE certificate. I suppose we both accepted that we had parents that were not quite the same as other people's parents.

Judy and Monika

Nearly seventy years later we are still talking. Between us we have brought up seven sons and we have sixteen grandchildren. We have sought each others' advice and support with adolescent boys and ailing parents. We have shared many triumphs and joys.

The one subject we seemed to avoid for so many years was the story of our early childhood years. Slowly, in many conversations, we learned about each others' lives.

afterwords

Monika

Once I was at St. Paul's I felt that I had won my spurs. My beloved stepfather adopted me and I became Monika Wandstein, a name I wrote proudly on all my beautiful exercise books. Once inside the school building, we did not need to wear a uniform, though the uniform coats were obligatory once we were let out.

My father enquired how many dresses I should have, so that I had the same number as all the other girls. He was not to know that it was the high quality and fancy fabrics of those Saks NY dresses that was a problem. They were glaringly unsuitable for my school life and made me want to die of shame.

Not until we were old ladies swinging on a hammock in Chile, did Judy begin to understand what an example of unattainable security she had been to me. Her clothes were right. She was comfortably sporty. She was Jewish, openly so, without a lump in her throat when she admitted it and seemed to have all sorts of interesting activities around her synagogue. I had never set foot in a synagogue, knew nothing of Hebrew. Jews did not pray in Latin. How often I pretended that I knew what she was talking about!

The routine of a well run school suited me. It all passed in a haze of pleasure: the excitement of concerts, the tension of exams and the tennis coaching where even determination and gritted teeth brought me no perceptible skill. While Judy played lacrosse, I preferred cricket, though both games involved the peril of being hit on a budding bosom by a vicious little missile, otherwise known as the ball.

I was far from brilliant but I justified Miss Osborne's decision to take me in spite of my failure to understand the entrance exam. The big problem arose at the age of sixteen when we had to decide if we were to follow a language or a science stream. My Father had a thriving dental practice and told me that dentistry was a wonderful career for a woman. I would be able to organise my own timetable around marriage and children. It was portable for the next time I had to run and a next time there would surely be. I gave in and settled to hours of incomprehension.

The problem was big because I had no talent for science. I could get by in Biology and could draw pretty diagrams. Chemistry was difficult but Physics could have been written in runes for all the sense it made. As simple maths brought in Algebra and Geometry and littered my horizon with sines and cosines and calculus, I cried. I never solved a quadratic equation, could not see what happiness a quadratic equation added to the human condition and still feel the scars of their unsolved triumph. Then one day I decided that I had suffered enough, walked into my parents' room at dawn and announced that I could do no more. I enrolled myself at a polytechnic and in seven months achieved excellent marks in my English, French and Latin A level exams.

At university I read English and other than the dreaded Beowulf, it was bliss. I made my life difficult, however, by marrying and having my first son before sitting for my degree. The fact that he cried most hours of the day and most of the night gave me time to read as I rocked him with my other hand, but for all that I had a miserable baby and achieved a miserable degree at the end of the sleepless nights. Two more sons followed and they were a full time job.

When the third son was about two years old, a good friend Ruth Sands, brought round three old children's books she had picked up on her travels. There was a whole history of childhood in those books and we began to look for more. We started to read the history of the attitude to childhood and to children. That children should be delighted was a comparatively modern concept and so the making of books for their pleasure was new. The books for their education were much older and so often consisted of just rote learning of countries and rivers as well as much emphasis on sin and how to avoid it.

Soon we realised that we had to sell some books in order to buy others. We typed a catalogue with our treasures and gave ourselves a name, M&R Glendale, because she lived in Glenilla Road and I lived in Daleham Gardens. We did not realize that Glendale placed us firmly in a town in California which we had never heard of, leading to constant denials with customers. After a few years, we rented a stand in an antique market. We learnt, looked and made mistakes. Interest in children's lives led inevitably to the women who brought them up and the governesses who taught them and to a whole new world of books about them, many written by celibate clergymen with a misogynist axe to grind. How galling it was to read that a girl may learn no more Latin than is needed to help her brother and the instructions at the bedroom door of a safely married woman was that she submit to all her husband's wishes. Ruth and I made friends round the world, exhibited at book fairs in the U.S.A and in Europe. When we finally had a shop of our own it became a meeting place for friends and family as well as for cranks of all sorts who assumed that a woman in an antiquarian bookshop must run a sideline in psychiatry.

All went well until our lease expired and we were offered a new one at nearly four times the previous rent. We packed our books and left as did the butcher, the baker and the candlestick maker, leaving their empty shops in our high street to the banks, estate agents and merchants of frilly dresses.

We had kept a day book in our shop and I raided all the comments and reflections, not always of the kindest, to write a memoir of our bookselling lives. We called it 'Don't Forget to Lock it Away.'

As the years passed, the boys grew from children to stroppy teenagers to perfectly delightful young men. We now have daughters-in-law, adding a new dimension to our male dominated lives. Judy even has some granddaughters, where I continued with another generation of short pants and seven-a-side football. As life flowed by, I lived it without noticing the speed of the flow, as most of us live. My parents died within five years of each other. My marriage collapsed. There followed years of great joy and much sadness.

Twenty two years ago I went to Chile for the first time with the man who later became my husband. It was the stated destination on the passports my Mother and I held when we left Poland. The Santiago of today is a fairly sophisticated city. Fifty years ago it was not; how my Mother would have hated it, she who loved cafés and window shopping and pretty clothes. Yet another reason to be grateful that she met my stepfather, married and stayed in London.

Today I live in Chile most of the year. It is my home, it is where I keep my books. I live half way up a mountain with humming birds and kestrels and an owl next to the kitchen door as my immediate neighbour.

Judy and I never lost touch. She was present for me throughout the black patches, never judging or criticising when I sometimes fell into holes of my own making. I hope that I was as much use to her as she was to me. The triumphs, big and small, we shared with satisfaction, be it birthday parties, weddings or prizes. Now that we are old ladies, just a little sentimentality may be permitted; how wonderful that after sixty eight years we should be looking back together and realising that for all our very different stories, we had so much in common.

Previously published work:

La Bambina sotto la Tavola
(Italian edition of the original letter to Eddie)

Don't Forget to Lock it Away—tales of fiction, friction and friendship (with Ruth Sands)

From My War to Your Peace, love Nonna—a letter to my grandson

Judy

In six years at St. Paul's I learned how to succeed academically. Not realizing it at the time, I must also have absorbed skills that later enabled me to work with deadlines or to start new ventures—and stick to them. Perhaps this came from the discipline of lessons, homework and end of term exams. It wasn't hard to enjoy all this because I was enthusiastic about the work, interspersed with sports which I loved. I arrived early to play tennis before school began. Shortcomings on the netball court or the lacrosse field were ironed out, till happily I was chosen to be in a couple of teams.

I had less success in art and music. On the top floor of the building there was an airy art studio. There I struggled to complete a decent portrait or landscape. The teacher didn't hestitate to tell me I simply had no talent. St. Paul's was known as a school with a strong musical tradition yet I never learned to play an instrument or to read music. I walked past the dozens of practice rooms, each equipped with a piano, feeling envious. In the singing hall we had illustrious teachers, including Herbert Howells the composer, who became our Director of Music. He trained our voices and inspired us to sing, but assumed that everyone could read a score, so my contribution to the school choir must have been minimal. Four decades later I was cajoled into joining a choir preparing to sing Handel's Messiah. There was still the problem of my inadequate knowledge of music theory but the joy of creating a complex sound from a hundred voices and joining in the final performance was one I will never forget.

Looking back at St. Paul's now, I wonder if it was considered 'character building' to play down academic achievement and offer sharp criticism of everything from posture to painting. It didn't occur to me then but perhaps I would have felt more confident in a co-ed school. Apart from meeting a few of David's friends, I rarely spoke to a boy, but an accident of timetabling was soon to bring about a dramatic change in my life.

In the middle of the two-year A-level course, when my choice had been to study modern languages, I had to leave St. Paul's. For some reason the timetable for the coming year couldn't accommodate German, French and Italian, so I left to go to the Lycée Français de Londres. There I was introduced to classes conducted in French. I was so proud to be attempting a subject called 'philosophie' sitting at a desk in a room half filled with boys. It was surprising that our work was unaffected by the hours spent languishing in the coffee bars of South Kensington. The year of my seventeenth birthday was momentous: I passed my exams with top marks and won a State Scholarship, a financial award for university entrants.

At the same time I made one of the biggest mistakes of my life. In spite of my parents' cajoling, but unbelievably little interference, I decided not to try for Oxford or Cambridge. My decision to forgo a university education was based on the mistaken belief that it would involve much medieval French. A preferable alternative was to start earning a living straight away. After a bilingual secretarial course, I got my first job as a translator and went on to work for several companies using mainly French and Italian.

The most important thing in my life happened in 1961 when I married Michael Jackson. We have been together for fifty seven years, longer and happier than I could ever have imagined. We have four sons (the last one arriving eighteen years after the first one was born).

When the first three were small I abandoned the idea of continuing the translation work and started a small catering business, which could be operated from home. Looking back I wonder how I had the nerve to do this. My knowledge of cooking was based on just a few years of practice. In our teens David used to protest if I tried to cook anything saying 'Don't bother, Mum does it much better.' So how did I learn? I enjoyed making soup and realized that success in that didn't depend on careful weighing or measuring. So when I married, soup was virtually the only thing I could cook. On my return from honeymoon a present arrived from my mother: a large illustrated volume, Marguerite Patten's 'Cookery in Colour'. I worked through the recipes and very quickly learned to make new dishes as well as how to find details of food we had eaten at home. Any skill I had came from years of absorbing techniques by standing in my mother's kitchen, watching what she did and finding out how things should look and taste.

The fastest way to close a business is to stop communicating with your customers. I moved house and 'forgot' to tell people where I had gone, but reignited my interest in cookery by offering classes to small groups in my new home. Thinking up new creations led to my believing that I could write a book. Incredibly, my first cookbook was accepted by the publisher Faber. More cookbooks followed along with food articles in several newspapers.

At about the same time I became a lay magistrate in Westminster, spending a day a week in court, dealing with everything from serious crime to motoring offences.

Twelve years ago I began to write novels. The first one, *The Camel Trail*, is based on the true story of a Portuguese ancestor, who was orphaned after an earthquake in the Middle East that killed his whole family. As I was unable to separate my interest in food from the novel writing, I included a brief recipe before each chapter. Because of this it was judged Best Food Literature Book in UK in 2008. I expect there were very few entries in this category!

The plot of the second novel was conceived on a long haul flight. *Sextet* is about relationships and music. It's the story of an illicit love affair that brings tragedy to the lives of six people.

Today my time is spent writing a food blog called *The Armchair Kitchen*, which involves photography, cooking and writing. It goes out four times a week and is followed by thousands of young people in the 18-24 age bracket. I think they like the pictures but don't cook the food! Last year I decided to visit Monika in Chile where she lives. In the week we shared together we had hours of discussion; sitting outdoors under the shade of a swing seat, floating in a pool, taking a short trip up the coast near Valparaiso. Inevitably much of the conversation was about the past. We have been talking, complaining, laughing and crying for sixty eight years. For much of that time we were separated by oceans, so face to face meetings were supplemented by hundreds of emails.

Tentatively I put to her the idea that I would like to combine the story of my childhood with the devastating episodes in her early years. It sounded almost unfeasible. The account of her early life had already been written. Mine would be far less dramatic and could be summarised in a few sentences. As I began to do more research into World War II and to search my memory for things that happened to me, everything suddenly became clearer. It was like the days after my cataract operation, as if a thin cloud had been removed from my eyes, but in this case it was the memories that started flooding back.

I am well aware that my recollections bear no comparison with Monika's, nor do the events we have both described have any equivalent weight. What we've both learned is that little girls can be embarrassed and humiliated and can also learn to deal with whatever 'normal life' seemed to offer.

I have thirteen grandchildren, ranging in age from twenty-six down to three. They live in America, Israel and London. The older ones all know Monika. Some have heard me mention her story. I hope that this account of two very different childhoods will make them reflect on their own early lives. They will surely be thankful that they have not lived in the shadow of war.

Previously published work:

The Home Book of Jewish Cookery

Microwave Vegetable Cooking

The Jewish Cookbook

A Feast in Fifteen Stories—a new start for hesitant cooks

Lookit Cookit—kitchen games for curious children

The Camel Trail

Sextet

Website: www.thearmchairkitchen.com

Food blog: www.lookitcookit.tumblr.com

The End

photographs

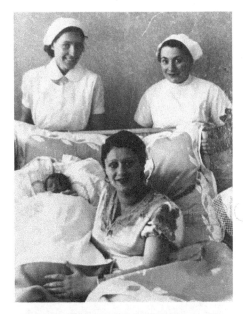

*Monika's birth in
Lódz 15th
February 1939*

*Judith c 1942
with her brother
David Blackburn
in the garden of her
grandmother's house
in Finchley*

Monika c 1948—a bridesmaid at the wedding of one of her father's patients

Monika with her grandmother, mother and new father on the first day at the Causeway school, Horsham, 8th January 1947

*Judith and David
c 1946 in fancy dress,
as Sir Walter Raleigh
and Queen Elizabeth*

*Monika at the
front door of the
Causeway School,
with a uniform
hat but still
wearing the camel
hair coat. 1948*

Monika with her thick plaits still in place at the age of 11 c 1950

Judy (top centre) and Monika (front left) with school friends including Rosalind Goldstein (top right) c 1950

Monika looking suitably serious in her first grown up tweed suit c 1955

Judy, wearing a sequinned dress made by her mother, with David at a dance party c 1954

*Judy and David's
mother Tess Blackburn
(probably in her fifties)*

*Their father
Rudolph Blackburn
(probably in his late sixties)*

*Monika in Italy,
dancing with a
young man long
since forgotten 1958*

*Judy and
Michael
on their
wedding
day 25th
June 1961*

Judy and Monika sometime in the 1980s

Judy and Michael's four sons c 1981

From left: Tim, David, Daniel and baby Adam

Judy and Michael at their oldest son Daniel's wedding in New York, 2nd April 1989

Adam with his three brothers on his wedding day in New York, 19th August 2007

*Pola (Apolonia)
Binkowska, Monika's
other Auntie who looked
after her at great risk
through much of the war*

*Judy and
Monika
at Adam's
wedding*

Monika outside an ice cream shop in Italy with her three sons
Oliver, Ian and Paul c 1995

Judy and Michael with their sons in Israel
for the batmitzvah of their granddaughter Shoshana in 2012

A joyous moment for Monika and her husband Carlos 2009

*Judy and Monika on a swing seat outside their home
in Pirque, Chile 2016*

historical notes

Judy

As background to what you have just read, here are some notes on significant events in England and Poland before and during World War II:

Having annexed Austria and occupied Czechoslovakia in 1938, in March 1939 Germany demanded that Gdansk should become part of Germany. Britain and France then pledged to defend Poland against attack.

In August Hitler and Stalin agreed a non-aggression pact, and secretly planned to divide Poland between them. Britain then signed a pact promising to defend Poland in the event of an attack 'by some European country.'

Between April and June 1940 Germany invaded and occupied Norway, Denmark, Luxemberg, Holland, Belgium and France. In May the German army trapped the British Expeditionary Force near Dunkirk. Nearly 340,000 Allied soldiers stranded on the beach were rescued by a fleet of over 800 small boats sent from England.

In June a large part of the Polish Air Force was moved to England, and the Polish Government in Exile moved to London.

In preparation for an invasion of England, the Luftwaffe began the Battle of Britain in July, fighting for air supremacy against the RAF. One in eight of the RAF pilots was Polish.

In 1941 Hitler launched Operation Barbarossa in clear breach of the Hitler-Stalin pact of 1939. A German force of four million troops pushed east across Poland to invade the Soviet Union. The Prime Minister of the Polish Government in Exile signed a treaty with the Soviet Union.

In 1944 Allied forces—British, American, Canadian and Free French— invaded Normandy in the D-day landings. This was the largest seaborne invasion in history. It began the liberation of German-occupied France (and later Europe) from Nazi control and laid the foundations of the Allied victory on the Western Front.

the timeline

preface—Judy

This timeline is not comprehensive. The selection of events is subjective: some shed light on the authors' personal stories; others highlight the prevailing atmosphere in the two countries.

Some universally known facts are omitted: for example Neville Chamberlain's ultimatum to Hitler and his subsequent broadcast to the British people. The fighting in Europe and North Africa is not documented. Not every Nazi camp in Poland is mentioned.

This is the only part of the book that was not written with input and discussion from both authors. I have compiled the Timeline. Research into the six years of war gave an insight into both the small concerns and the greater fears of the British people at that time. In documenting the Polish part I have discovered details of the horrors unfolding as the war progressed. Monika preferred not to contribute to selecting the events, or to editing these pages.

1939

24 August
Parliament is
recalled to grant
the government
special powers 'for
the duration of
the crisis'. Army
reservists are called
up.

3 June
All men aged 20-21 are liable to
call up for military service.

Britain

Poland

25 February
Warsaw students
demonstrate
in front of the
German Embassy.

30 April
A visiting group from
the Polish Theatre of
Katowice are beaten by
a Nazi crowd in Oppein,
Gross Strehlitz, a town in
SW Poland.

3 September
Britain declares war on Germany.

1 September
In response to the German invasion of Poland and the prospect of war with Germany, plans are made to evacuate children from London and other big cities. The first evacuee children leave Stepney in London at 5 am. The Blackout begins. The British Army is officially mobilized.

6 October
The 'Phoney War' begins and lasts till April 1940, with little military action. The French call it 'Drôle de guerre' (funny war) and the Germans 'Sitzkrieg' (sitting war).

1 November
London schools start to reopen as evacuee children return to the capital.

1 September
Germany invades Poland from the West.

3 September
Bloody Sunday. German and Polish civilians fight for the city of Bromberg. 800 Polish hostages are shot in a mass execution. The Germans occupy the city and kill nearly 3000 Polish citizens.

6 November
A German operation is conducted against university professors in German occupied Krakau. 184 academics, invited to attend a lecture, are arrested on the spot, imprisoned, and sent to Sachsenhausen concentration camp. Many do not survive.

6 October
Poland is now under complete occupation by Germany and the Soviet Union.

17 September
The Soviet Union invades Poland from the East.

1940

14 May
The Home Guard (Dad's Army) is created from local defence volunteers.

10 May
After Hitler's invasion of France, Churchill becomes Prime Minister.

23 May
Evacuation begins of British and French armies from the beaches of Dunkirk. By 28 May 340,000 troops have been ferried to England.

8 January
Food rationing is introduced.

14 June
France surrenders.

30 June
German troops occupy the Channel Islands (Crown Dependencies).

Britain

Poland

May
The Red Army execute 22,000 Polish officers and intellectuals in the Katyn Forest. Ukrainians, Belarusians and Polish Jews, including the Chief Rabbi of the Polish Army, are also killed.

25 January
Construction of the Auschwitz concentration camp begins near the Polish village of Oswiecim.

30 April
230,000 Jews are sealed inside the Lódz ghetto.

5 March
Joseph Stalin orders the execution of 25,700 Polish 'nationalists and counter-revolutionaries'.

25 February
Polish students demonstate in front of the German Embassy in Warsaw.

12 February
The Nazis begin deporting German Jews to Poland.

7 September
The Blitz begins. London is bombed for 57 consecutive days and nights.

25-28 August
Major air raids on Birmingham and Liverpool.

10 September
Evacuated from their homes in a bomb scare, 600 civilians die, bombed while sheltering for three days in the basement of a school in Canning Town, E London. Reporting is suppressed to prevent demoralisation and unrest.

31 October
The Battle of Britain ends.

9 July
Start of the Battle of Britain.

14 November
A massive German bombing raid on Coventry destroys 4,300 homes and damages two thirds of the buildings and one third of the factories in the city centre.

November
70,000 Polish Jews are sealed inside the Krakow ghetto.

15 November
400,000 Polish Jews are sealed inside the Warsaw ghetto. The only way for the starving occupants to survive is through smuggling food. Nonetheless, the Jews set up libraries, childrens' classes, and an orchestra.

1941

13 March German bombing of the shipbuilding area of Clydebank in Glasgow kills 528, seriously injures 617 and leaves 35,000 homeless.

2-8 May
German bombing of the docks in Merseyside, Liverpool, kills 1,700 and injures 4,000.

9 May
The Royal Navy captures a German submarine in the North Atlantic, along with its Enigma cryptograph machine and German Navy codebooks.

May
Luftwaffe bombing decreases in intensity. The period of two and a half years to January 1944 is known as 'The Lull'.

1 June
Clothes rationing begins.

Poland

30 June
Pogroms start in Lvov in occupied eastern Poland. German commandos and Ukrainian nationalists kill around 6,000 Jews.

10 July
Jedwabne. German police and 40 ethnic Poles lock 340 Polish Jews in a barn. All the men, women and children die when it is set it on fire.

2 July
In Lvov, 25 Polish academics and their familes are killed by Einsatzgruppen, including Ukrainians dressed in German uniforms.

18 December
National Service becomes compulsory for all men and women aged 18-60.

8 December
The Japanese attack Pearl Harbour and invade Hong Kong. Britain declares war on Japan.

5 December
Britain declares war on Germany's allies Finland, Hungary and Romania.

November
Lvov ghetto is established.
120,000 Jews are deported to Belzec concentration camp. Only 823 of them find their way back to the city.

12 October
German SS squads, with Ukrainian police, dig mass graves at the Jewish cemetery in Stanislawow.
Dr. Tenenbaum, head of the Judenrat, is offered exemption from the planned execution; he refuses and is killed along with 10,000 -12,000 other Jews.

3 September
Zyklon-B gas is first tested at Auschwitz.

1942

Britain

10 January
Bombing in Liverpool kills Hitler's half brother Alois.

7 February
Soap rationing is introduced.

May
Cost of a restaurant meal in Britain is restricted to a maximum of 5 shillings per person.

30 May
The RAF attacks Cologne in the first thousand-bomber raid. Canterbury is bombed in reprisal.

4 September
The Paper Control order comes into effect. Paper shortage hampers publishers and authors. Wrapping paper is prohibited.

Poland

19 July
After the assassination of Reinhard Heydrich, Himmler orders the mass deportation of Polish Jews to concentration camps.

22 July
Liquidation of the Warsaw Ghetto begins. The Jews of Warsaw are deported to Treblinka, which becomes an operational extermination camp the following day.

May
Sobibor concentration camp becomes operational.

17 March
The Jews of Lublin are deported to Belzec concentration camp.

January
Regular mass exterminations begin at Auschwitz-Birkenau.

13 September
The RAF carries out its 100th bombing raid on Bremen in Germany.

25 October
The milk ration is
cut to two and a
half pints a week.

November
Under The Utility Furniture
Scheme new furniture is rationed
and restricted to newly-weds and
those from bombed homes.

29th October
At a public
meeting the
Archbishop of
Canterbury and
international
political figures
express outrage at
the Holocaust.

17 December
Britain officially addresses the massacre
of the Jews by Germans in occupied
Europe. Foreign Secretary Anthony
Eden condemns 'this bestial policy of
cold blooded extermination' and the
transport of hundreds of thousands of
Jews to Eastern Europe 'in conditions of
appalling horror and brutality.'

8 October
The Polish Home Army destroys
Warsaw's main railway yards.

1943

20 January
Sandhurst Road School in Catford, SE London, is bombed. 38 children and 6 teachers are killed.

3 March
Air raid panic causes a crush at Bethnel Green tube station, killing 183.

March
In the battle of the Atlantic, German U-boats sink 27 merchant ships of a single convoy.
The British people are told that enormous losses have been inflicted on the U-boats by the use of long-range aircraft and codebreaking intelligence.

Britain

Poland

14 March
The Krakow Ghetto is liquidated.

9 April
Exterminations at the Chelmno concentration camp are temporarily halted. They resume a year later.

19 April
The Warsaw Ghetto Uprising, led by Mordecai Anielewicz, is the first civilian uprising in occupied Europe. A Jewish resistance group drives back SS troops attempting the final annihilation of the Ghetto. The Jews fight for three weeks with few weapons, stones, knives and even fists. 7,000 Jewish fighters are killed.

8 May
The remaining leaders of the Jews commit suicide.
56,000 surviving inmates are deported to Treblinka for extermination.

11 May
Himmler orders liquidation of the remaining Jewish Ghettos in Poland.

17 August
The RAF bombs Peenemunde in Germany. This Baltic sea island is the site for the development of V-1 and V-2 rockets.

16 November
Villages are evacuated in Salisbury Plain and Devon, to make way for a rehearsal of the planned invasion of German occupied Europe.

26 November
A British troopship is sunk off the North Africa coast by a radio controlled glide bomber, killing 1,015.

25 December
At the end of this year when virtually every household item has been in short supply or unavailable, the British are used to queueing. At one shop with 800 registered customers, there are just 3 Christmas puddings on sale.

December
Work on the Colossus computer is completed at the Post Office Research Station, Dollis Hill, N London. It is designed to speed up cryptanalysis at Bletchley Park, the centre for code breaking operations.

October
Treblinka is closed. 870,000 victims have been killed there.

14 October
300 Jews and Soviet POWs escape from Sobibor concentration camp. The camp is closed, dismantled and the grounds planted over to hide evidence of 250,000 victims.

2 August
At Treblinka those forced to bury the bodies (the Sonderkommando) revolt and kill several guards. 200 prisoners escape from the camp.

4 July
Wladyslaw Sikorski, Prime Minister of the Polish government in exile, is killed in an air crash near Gibraltar.

1944

Britain

22 January
Operation Steinbock, nicknamed The Baby Blitz, begins. The Luftwaffe mount a night bombing offensive against Greater London. Few German aircraft reach their targets. 329 of 474 machines are lost.

5 June
The scheduled day for the Normandy Landings. Weather conditions force postponement to the following day. A coded message is sent to French resistance groups.

6 June
Operation Overlord. 155,000 Allied troops (British, American, Canadian and French) cross the Channel to Normandy. Australian and New Zealand Air Forces and the Royal Norwegian Navy contribute air and sea support. The Allies establish control of five Normandy beaches.

11 June
325,000 Allied troops, 54,000 vehicles and 570,000 tons of supplies have been landed. Polish, Czechoslovak, Belgian, Greek and Dutch troops eventually participate in the fighting.

13 June
The first flying bomb (V-1) attack on London. The V-1 is nicknamed the Doodlebug.

Poland

28 February
1,000 Polish inhabitants of the village Huta Pieniacka are massacred with extreme brutality. The village was a stronghold of Polish resistance to German and Ukrainian forces.

April
Polish resistance Armia Krajowa informs British Intelligence of V-2 rocket tests at Blizna. They retrieve rocket parts for analysis in secret laboratories in Warsaw.

20 June
Searching for Polish partisans, Lithuanian police attack Glinciszki village. Many civilians are murdered, including 12 women and 11 children. Members of Armia Krajowa are killed in a shootout with the Lithuanians.

July/August
Further raids on the Peenemunde rocket launch site fail to
stop the flying bombs.

12 August
After 60 days the
V-1 bombs have
killed 6,000,
injured 17,000,
and damaged
or destroyed
a million
buildings.

25 November
A V-2 rocket kills
168 people in a
Woolworths store in
S London.

8 September
The first V-2 rocket attack strikes
Chiswick in London.

1 August
In Warsaw the Polish Armia Krajowa rebel against German
occupation. The British send supplies, with the RAF making 200
low-level drops. Stalin and Roosevelt refuse to help the Poles.

24 July
An RAF plane lands
near Lublin; partisans
hand over V-2 missile
parts. The plane returns
to London and delivers
its cargo to British
scientists.

1945

13 February
Bombing raids begin on Dresden, Germany. Thousands of civilians die in the firestorm created by 1,300 Allied bombers.

27 March
Last V-1 flying bomb kills 134 people in Stepney E London.

15 April
British troops liberate Bergen-Belsen concentration camp in Germany. The soldiers find 60,000 half-starved prisoners and 13,000 unburied corpses. Richard Dimbleby's report reveals the Holocaust to the British public.

8 May
Germany surrenders unconditionally. The Allies declare Victory in Europe, 8 days after Hitler's suicide.

26 July
Labour victory in the UK general election is announced. Clement Attlee replaces Winston Churchill as Prime Minister.

Poland

3 March
In Pawlokoma groups of Poles massacre hundreds of Ukrainians.

17 July
Churchill and Attlee, Truman and Stalin begin the Potsdam Conference. Principles are agreed for the treatment of Germany. Territorial changes are agreed for Poland, and some reparations for Polish damage suffered in the war. The Provisional Government of National Unity is recognised.

12 July
The Soviet Union takes over Poland. The Red Army attacks Polish World War II anti-communist partisans.

27 June
In Krakow false rumours circulate that a Jewish woman has abducted a child to kill it. Blood libels and other false accusations follow. Crowds repeatedly stone the Kupa Synagogue.

8 May
End of World War II in Europe.

188

6 August
The first atomic bomb is dropped on Hiroshima, killing 200,000.

9 August
The second Atomic bomb is dropped on Nagasaki, killing 200,000.

16 August
Winston Churchill is now Leader of the Opposition in Parliament. In a speech he says that an 'Iron Curtain' is descending across Europe.

2 September
Japan surrenders. Wartime press censorship ends.

December
Alexander Fleming and Ernst Chain win the Nobel Prize for the discovery of penicillin.

31 December
Britain receives its first shipment of bananas since the beginning of the war.

11 August
A pogrom takes place in Krakow. Of 80,000 living there before the war, 2,000 Jews remain. By May another 4,000 have returned from the Soviet Union. During the Sabbath morning service a crowd breaks into the synagogue. The Torah scrolls are burned, people beaten on the streets, homes broken into and robbed. Those taken to hospital are attacked again when they are discharged. One person dies in the violence: a 56-year old Auschwitz survivor.

Printed in January 2022
by Rotomail Italia S.p.A., Vignate (MI) - Italy